The Basics of the Faith

By Mark A. Pearson

First Printing.
Latimer Press
30325 Bainbridge Road
Building A, Suite 1
Solon, Ohio 44139

Also by Mark A. Pearson:

Christian Healing: A Practical, Comprehensive Guide
(Chosen Books, 1990)

Why Can't I Be Me? Understanding How Personality Type Affects: Emotional Healing, Relationships, Spiritual Growth
(Chosen Books, 1992)

Dedication

To my children
Stephen
Jennifer
Michael

May God's grace help them
to understand and practice
the basics of the faith

Contents

Preface

I became a member of the Episcopal Church as a high-school student in 1965. I had been raised in the Congregational Church but was increasingly hungry for something more. In my mostly ethnic, blue-collar, Roman Catholic, Democrat city, these Congregational people were like me: WASP, middle-class, Protestant, Republican. To go to Church was like being part of an extended family. I was with many people like myself, and they were good people. But that's how the Church was defined — good people, socioeconomically and ethnically similar, enjoying each other's company. It had very little to do with the spiritual life. I was increasingly hungry for God.

Over the years my father had told me stories of the Episcopal men and boys choir in which he had sung while growing up one city to the north. His father had sung in that choir for 54 years, his uncles and brothers had sung in it, and his grandfather started singing in it when he came to this country from Canada in 1897. This was a wonderful heritage and it appealed to my romantic, sentimental side. Additionally, four of my male cousins were now singing in that choir, and I was jealous!

Although I was proud to be an American, I was also an Anglophile, and what my relatives were telling me about the Episcopal Church seemed to indicate that it was Anglophile, too. One day I asked the master of that choir, a man who had also become my organ teacher, if I could sing in the choir on Christmas Eve. In the persons of those four cousins the family was already into the fourth generation of singing in this venerable choir. I had to have this for me, too.

That Christmas Eve was everything I had hoped for. I had now sung in the choir I had invested with so much meaning. I was now part of that fourth generation of choir singers going back to 1897. I reveled in the Englishness of the whole experience. I had expected to have a good time that Christmas Eve, and I certainly did.

One thing I had not expected that Christmas Eve was my falling in love with Anglicanism. I was caught up in the reality of God's majestic transcendence. I saw how people were either in prayer or in reverent silence before the service started. I observed how people reverenced the altar as they passed in front of it. I noted how the Creed was presented as the objective truth of the faith, not something merely cultural or negotiable. I was taken with how many teenagers and young adults were present, and how the faith was important to them. And I discovered *The Book of Common Prayer*.

As I leafed through the Prayer Book I was taken by the Catechism. Here was a series of questions and answers, with the questions addressing themselves to basic issues of the faith. The answers were straightforward, simple and uncompromised. There was no hint here of the kinds of statements I had heard in my home church: "It doesn't matter what you believe," "There are no real objective answers true for everyone," and "All that counts is being nice to one another."

I fell in love with Anglicanism that Christmas Eve of 1964. I so appreciated the reverence before God; the belief that the Church was centered on God, not one's social group; and the unapologetic declaration of the truths of the faith.

I'm glad I started reading the Prayer Book and discovered Anglicanism was based on theological truths, not merely on being formal, English, or cultured. Had I not discovered those truths, my desire to become Episcopalian would have been just a swap of one religious social club (Yankee and informal) for another (English and ceremonial). Indeed, there are many for whom the Episcopal Church is just a rather cultured, upscale social club and nothing more. But in discovering the content of the faith, especially as expressed in the Catechism, I found that the content of the faith mattered. It wasn't something we made up as we went along or changed as we felt like it, but was given by God, was real, true, and objective.

On the way home from the Christmas Eve service I told my parents I wanted to be part of that Episcopal Church. My father was ready to return to the Episcopal Church as he, too, was increasingly troubled by the believe-anything-you-want attitude of liberal Protestantism. My mother wasn't so sure at first. In any case, that next Sunday we were in the Episcopal Church.

Our Congregational pastor, a kindly elderly man, was of course sad to see us go. In talking with my parents, he uttered thoughts that proved to be most prophetic. Addressing my father, he said words to this effect: The Episcopal Church you are going back to in 1965 is not the Episcopal Church you left when you got married in 1944. You are concerned with the growing denial of the historic faith in the Congregational Church. What you don't realize is that the Episcopal Church has embarked on the same journey. You will find in the years ahead that the Episcopal Church will most likely accelerate the turn from the historic faith for liberalism, both in theology and in morality.

How prescient he was! We are observing an erosion of the integrity of the Church by the false teachings, outrageous actions and, in many cases, immoral actions of many Church leaders. The Church is increasingly turning from God's doctrinal and moral teachings for things specifically ruled out by Scripture.

At this time of crisis and confusion we need a reassertion of the basics of the faith. I believe this is true for three reasons.

First, because God gives the contents of the faith. Simply put, disciples are people who believe what God said, regardless of whether we fully understand it or like it. To call oneself a follower of Christ and not believe this theological and moral teaching is a contradiction in terms. You cannot be a believer on your own terms.

Second, because of the questions that are in the minds of so many laypeople as they listen to confusing and contradictory statements by Church leaders.

Third, because many who have come to the Lord through one or another renewal ministry need to have their experience undergirded by sound teaching. Many have come to the Lord through a profound experience of God during a Faith Alive weekend, a Cursillo retreat, participation in a charismatic prayer meeting, an Anglican Fellowship of Prayer conference, or some other event. Their excitement is real, their newness in Christ is genuine, their thrill is palpable.

Unless that experience is undergirded by solid, basic teaching, people will eventually cool off and go back to the spiritual dullness that they had known before their experiences of the Lord, or they will bounce from experience to experience with no rootedness, or they will discover their relationship with the Lord either is not growing or it is growing in a distorted, false way.

This book, expanding on the Catechism of *The Book of Common Prayer* (1979), is designed to speak to these three points.

The Anglican heritage and its Catechism are precious gifts of God. As you read this book, I hope you, too, will fall in love with these gifts in a new or deeper way.

Mark A. Pearson
Plaistow, New Hampshire

Introduction

I have written this book to set forth the basics of the faith. We may embrace a diversity of spiritual styles, but to be authentic Christians we must believe a number of foundational doctrines. We will look at these in the first part of this book. (For a study of the diversity of legitimate spiritual styles, see my book *Why Can't I Be Me?*)

Similarly, while we may choose from among several legitimate methods of Bible study, prayer, discerning God's will, and evangelism, all Christians must engage in these spiritual disciplines. We will look at these in the second part of this book.

Perhaps you have been a loyal son or daughter of the Church all your life but want a brief refresher course on the basics. Perhaps you have been part of the Church but know there are gaps in your spiritual education. Perhaps you have just experienced a spiritual "high," a time of new or renewed relationship with God, and want to ground it in solid Biblical teaching and spiritual practice. Perhaps you are not sure of the Christian faith and want to examine the central core of Christianity without the distraction of peripheral issues.

I've written this book for people in any of these circumstances.

I will quote various passages of Scripture in each chapter of this book. I also will quote from the Catechism. Throughout its history, the Christian Church has set forth creeds and catechisms as summary statements of the faith. The title of the Catechism found in *The Book of Common Prayer* (see p. 845) is instructive:

An Outline of the Faith
commonly called the Catechism

At the end of each chapter I've included several discussion questions to help groups study this book. I've also recommended several books for the reader seeking further study.

Most of the authors are Anglican — which doesn't imply that members of other churches cannot write good books. Rather, since I've written this book especially for Episcopalians, I've emphasized books written by members of the Anglican Communion.

1

What is the Gospel?

We must start with that most foundational of all questions confronting the human race: What is God's basic message to the human race? For purposes of this study, I will summarize the Gospel in four propositions.

1. God's desire for everyone is a joyous, fulfilled life lived in perfect fellowship with Him.

"I came that they may have life, and have it abundantly."[1]

Q. What are we by nature?
A. We are part of God's creation, made in the image of God.

Q. What does it mean to be created in the image of God?
A. It means that we are free to make choices: to love, to create, to reason, and to live in harmony with creation and with God.[2]

This was God's intent for the human race from its origin. Look at Adam and Eve before their disobedience (Genesis 2) and see how true this is. Whether we take this account as literal or as figurative, the point is the same: The human race initially was happy, fulfilled, and free from sickness, pain, strife, and death.

---

[1]Jesus, speaking in John 10:10b
[2]Catechism, *The Book of Common Prayer*, p. 845, sets 1 and 2.

But something went wrong. We certainly do not have this carefree existence — this freedom from sickness, pain, strife, and death, or perfect fellowship with God. What went wrong?

2. We sinned, choosing our own ways instead of what God commanded.

Q. Why then do we live apart from God and out of harmony with creation?
A. From the beginning, human beings have misused their freedom and made wrong choices.

Q. Why do we not use our freedom as we should?
A. Because we rebel against God, and we put ourselves in the place of God.[3]

Q. What is sin?
A. Sin is the seeking of our own will instead of the will of God, thus distorting our relationship with God, with other people, and with all creation.[4]

Q. How does sin have power over us?
A. Sin has power over us because we lose our liberty when our relationship with God is distorted.[5]

In seeking to play God, we lost fellowship with God and one another. Our sin is what traditional theologians call "original," both because it comes from the beginning of the human race and because every human being is flawed by it as a spiritual inheritance. Our sin is also "actual," because we add our own sins to the sinful state we have inherited. The Bible tells us that this describes each person: "For all have sinned and fall short of the glory of God" (Romans 3:23). No one is exempt from the category of "sinner."

The consequences of our sin are manifold:

1. Sin dishonors God. When I was little my father told me that my misbehaving in public might bring disrepute on our family's good name. Similarly, our sin dishonors God before the world. We hold God up to mockery if people know we are Christians and see us behaving in ways contrary to our faith.

---

[3]Ibid., p. 845, sets 3 and 4.
[4]Ibid., p. 848, last set.
[5]Ibid., p. 849, first set.

2. Sin harms others. Clearly many of the sins committed in public harm others — but what about the activity of "consenting adults behind closed doors"? Even that behavior is harmful to others. Why?

Adults are not immune to harm just because they consent to an activity. When we participate in behavior contrary to God's will, we enable other people to commit sin. We also render ourselves less able to fulfill Christian responsibilities to others.

How? Let's look at just a few of the ways. Let's say we manage to show up for church Sunday morning in spite of a hangover from Saturday night. Let's say someone asks us to pray for her physical illness or give her spiritual counsel in a problem she is facing. We will not likely be spiritually sharp or able to be an instrument in God's hand.

More seriously, we may become tolerant of sin to quiet our guilty conscience. We may start to believe our "tolerance" is a case of our becoming more loving, more understanding or more inclusive, when actually we're turning our backs on the commandments of God. Such rationalizations keep us from speaking out against the sinful behavior of others. Deep down we know that our speaking out would be hypocritical, given our own sinful behaviors. So we remain silent. Our moral compromising has rendered us impotent in confronting sin, whether it is "tough love" intervention with a friend or a prophetic denunciation of the sins of society.

3. Sin harms us. Eventually the soul that persists in sinning drifts away from God. The soul becomes less a reflection of God and more a reflection of something God does not mean the soul to be. The divine image grows fainter and fainter. Even though such a person may be educated and sophisticated, accepted by society and hailed by peers, this person is lost.

There are physical consequences to sin. To give but one example, holding on to anger renders a person much more vulnerable to elevated blood pressure and all the physical problems stemming from it. While not all physical sickness is rooted in our own sinful actions or attitudes, some is.

Eventually, unless we are rescued from our sin we will be cut off from heaven for all eternity. This is a constant theme of Scripture and the motivating force behind the intensity of Jesus' preaching. As two scripture verses describe it, "The soul who sins is the one who will die" (Ezekiel 18:4) and "For the wages of sin is death" (Romans 6:23a, referring not only to physical death but also to spiritual death). Because every person sins, each person on earth lives under the death sentence of eternal lostness.

Some may argue this point. "Oh, I suppose there will be some people who will be eternally lost — rapists, murderers, people like Hitler. But I'm nowhere as bad as them." Some of us may compare ourselves with others. "But look at what I am compared to many people I know." These are easy conclusions to draw, but they are irrelevant.

God does not want us to compare ourselves with the achievements, activities, or even moral standings of others. Our comparison is over against the commandments He gave us. I once met a man who tried to convince me of how wonderful he was with all his religious observances and acts of decency. I asked if he would tell me how he was doing in just three particular areas. He agreed. I asked him:

Did he tithe? (Malachi 3:8)

Was he free from lusting after people in his heart? (Matthew 5:28)

Did he share his coats with those who had none? (Luke 3:11)

Reluctantly, he admitted he was not in conformity with any of the three. The standards God sets are high indeed, and no one can keep them. The standards are as they are because God is good and holy. But the standards also show us that *everyone* has fallen short, that *each person* needs a Saviour. Religiously superficial people loudly protest their innocence. Truly holy people quickly acknowledge how far short they are from what God wants, and how much they need the saving grace of God in Christ. As the Catechism says,

Q. Since we do not fully obey [God's commandments], are they useful at all?

A. Since we do not fully obey them, we see more clearly our sin and our need for redemption.[6]

The Good News of the Gospel is not that you are a sinner. That is not even news! The Good News is that God has done something about it.

3. Redemption is possible, not through who we are or what we do, but through what Christ has done for us.

Q. What is meant by the Messiah?

A. The Messiah is the one sent by God to free us from the power of sin, so that with the help of God we may live in harmony with God, within ourselves, with our neighbors, and with all creation.[7]

Q. What is the great importance of Jesus' suffering and death?

A. By his obedience, even to suffering and death, Jesus made the offering which we could not make; in him we are freed from the power of sin and reconciled to God.[8]

To understand that offering which makes possible eternal life, we have to trace what some have called "the thin red line of blood" through the Scriptures.

In Genesis 4:3-7, we read that Cain and Abel made presentations to God. Cain brought vegetables and Abel brought the blood of a sheep. To us they both look like good, sincere offerings, but God deemed only Abel's acceptable.

Why? First, because God is not capricious or cruel, we have to assume God told them already what was acceptable to Him. Abel chose to obey while Cain chose to do a good thing but in his own way.

Second, Cain and Abel are "types," or symbolic representatives of two kinds of people. Cain, bringing vegetables, was offering to God the fruits of his hands ("God, I am offering you something I did to earn your favor"). Cain symbolizes those who try to earn salvation through good works, or who think they're decent, or who think they can become

---

[6]Ibid., p. 848, set 2.

[7]Ibid., p. 849 set 4.

[8]Ibid., p. 850, set 2.

their own Saviour. Abel is the exemplar of those who come before the Lord with the offering God prescribes: shed blood, the life of the innocent offered up for the sins of the guilty.

Let us now "fast forward" to the Book of Exodus, Chapter 11. The children of Israel were in bondage in Egypt. Although God, through Moses, worked several miracles to persuade Pharaoh to let God's people go free, Pharaoh refused. God then told the Jews that an angel of death would visit the city. They were to take the blood of a lamb and smear it on the doorposts of their houses. When the angel of death saw the blood it would pass over that house, hence the term *Passover*.

Again, note the significance of the blood: death would come except where the blood was found. This is why the Jews kept the Passover celebration each year: to remind them that they could not come before God on their own merits, or with offerings of their own choosing, but with the only appointed offering, the shed blood of an innocent lamb. This is why throughout the Old Testament we see the Jews offering up lambs as sacrifice in worship.

Although this was what God appointed, it wasn't sufficient or complete. Why? As the Epistle to the Hebrews puts it (10:1-4), "The law is only a shadow of the good things that are coming — not the realities themselves. For this reason it can never, by the same sacrifices repeated endlessly year after year, make perfect those who draw near to worship. If it could, would they not have stopped being offered? For the worshipers would have been cleansed once for all, and would no longer have felt guilty for their sins. But those sacrifices are an annual reminder of sins, because it is impossible for the blood of bulls and goats to take away sins."

God the Father sent Jesus to be that sacrifice for sin to do what the Old Testament animal sacrifices could only foreshadow but never accomplish: pay the penalty of people's sins and make reconciliation with God possible. John the Baptist knew that Jesus would accomplish this for us. Pointing to Jesus, John declared, "Look, the Lamb of God, who takes away the sin of the world!" (John 1:29). Jesus knew His job was to go to the cross to take the penalty for our sins. Speaking of Himself in the third person, Jesus said His mission was "to give his life as a ransom for many" (Mark 10:45). On the cross Jesus bore the sins of the world, paying the penalty those sins incurred.

His sacrifice worked! Jesus paid in full the price for our sins. God the Father deemed Jesus' sacrifice worthy, and forgave us our sins. The historic Eucharistic prayer describes what Jesus accomplished on the cross: "who made there, by his one oblation of himself once offered, a full, perfect, and sufficient sacrifice, oblation, and satisfaction, for the sins of the whole world."[9]

4. To have the benefits of Calvary applied to us, we must receive Jesus Christ as Saviour and Lord.

It is not enough to know the truth of the Gospel intellectually. We have to receive it personally. (It was not enough for the Jews in Egypt to *know about* the angel of death or that God wanted blood put on the doorposts. They had to do it.) Put another way, it is not enough to know Jesus is *the* Saviour. The big question is, is He *yours*?

How do we receive this perfect gift of salvation that is necessary for eternal life and is available only through Jesus Christ? We receive it as we receive any other gift — by humbly taking it, by acknowledging our sinfulness and lostness and asking Jesus to bear the penalty of our sins as our Saviour.

Don't waste your time debating whether you've made this decision before. If you are not sure you have received Jesus as your Saviour, why not make sure? As the late Canon David C.K. Watson once said, "Perhaps years ago you asked Jesus to be your Saviour and you, as it were, wrote your name on the contract in pencil. Over the years that signature has faded, perhaps even been partially erased. Don't take a chance! If you want Jesus as your Saviour, take a pen and resign it in ink. God won't be angry at you for signing that contract more times than is necessary. But there are eternal consequences if you have never signed it. Why take that chance?"

---

[9]*The Book of Common Prayer*, p. 334.

By comparison, notice how the Church has, in her wisdom, made provision for "conditional baptism." If we are not sure a baby has been baptized, we baptize the baby using the words, "If you are not already baptized, *N.*, I baptize you in the Name of the Father, and of the Son, and of the Holy Spirit" (*The Book of Common Prayer*, p. 313). The point is that baptism is so important it is better to err on the side of doing it too often than on the side of not at all.

In a similar way, there is nothing wrong with asking Jesus to be Lord and Saviour even though you may have done so in some way at some time in the past. If you know right now that you are a sinner and cannot save yourself and want Jesus to be your Saviour, pray this simple prayer of dedication (or rededication):

> Heavenly Father, I admit to you that I am a sinner. I have not loved You with my whole heart. I have not loved my neighbor as myself. But You, O God, love me and have provided Jesus for my salvation to pay the penalty price for my sin. So now I receive that free gift of salvation made possible by Jesus taking my sin and guilt upon Him. I ask Jesus to be that Saviour I need. And I vow, by Your grace, to follow Him as my Lord and Master for the rest of my life. Thank you, Father, for my salvation. In Jesus' Name. Amen.

If you have sincerely asked Jesus Christ to be your Saviour and Lord, you need to know three things:

1. *Don't trust your feelings.* After praying this prayer some people feel elated, some people feel nothing, a few even feel dejected. C.S. Lewis said that right after he had given his life to Jesus, he felt like the most dejected convert in all of England. Feelings depend on many things, some beyond our control. Your salvation does not depend on feelings but on the truths of the Gospel and on the promise of God. Looking at Revelation 3:20 helps me. There we read a description of Jesus standing outside a door saying, "I stand at the door and knock. If anyone hears my voice and opens the door, I will come in and eat with him and he with me." By asking Jesus to be your Saviour and Lord you have opened that door. He has said He will enter in. Trust His promise and not your feelings.

2. *You will stumble.* When Christians sin, they do not lose their salvation, although sometimes there are temporal consequences of sin. We then need to go to the Lord, ask forgiveness for those sins we committed, receive

His forgiveness and work at growing in holiness. The Scriptural phrase "born again" is so instructive here (John 3:3). When we are babies we are complete human beings, not just 25 percent human. Yet we have so much growing to do. Likewise, as spiritual babies we are not just 25 percent Christians. We are Christians, period. But there's so much growing to do! (Later in this book we will look at various means of spiritual growth.)

3. *When we ask Jesus to come into our lives it is both as Saviour and Lord.* We do not ask Jesus to take the penalty of our sin so we can keep on sinning. Jesus doesn't offer cheap grace. Nor does He offer Himself as Saviour apart from being Lord. Rather, when we accept Jesus as Saviour, we also vow, by God's grace, to obey Him in all things. Our obedience is not, of course, to earn anything. Remember, we cannot earn our salvation. Our obedience, rather, is a heartfelt thank you to God for the salvation He freely gives us in Christ. As the Catechism says about our response to Christ's free gift of salvation:

> Q. What response did Christ require?
> A. Christ commanded us to believe in him and to keep his commandments.[10]

In the next three chapters we will examine the content of "believe in Him." In the last six chapters we will look at how we may grow spiritually and "keep His commandments."

DISCUSSION QUESTIONS:

1. Why do you think so many Church people remain so ignorant of the basic Gospel message?

2. How does human pride cause some to attack the Gospel of Christ and substitute another one?

3. The Bible says the religious person would be the hardest person to convince of the need of a Saviour. How is that true today?

---

[10]Catechism, *The Book of Common Prayer*, p. 851 set 2.

FOR FURTHER READING:

Carey, George, *I Believe*, Morehouse Publishing. (Carey is the 103rd Archbishop of Canterbury.)

Lewis, C. S., *Mere Christianity*, Collier Books.

Packer, James I., *I Want to Be a Christian*, Tyndale.

Stott, John R.W., *Men Made New*, Baker Books.

Stott, John R.W., *Basic Christianity*, InterVarsity Press.

2

The Trinity

Q. What is the Trinity?
A. The Trinity is one God: Father, Son, and Holy Spirit.[1]

The doctrine of the Trinity, one of the basic teachings of Christianity, states that God is one but has existed from all eternity as three Persons.

Christians do not believe in three Gods — that's polytheism.

We do not believe in one God (God the Father) with two lesser demigods — that's the heresy of subordinationism.

Nor do we believe in one God of one Person appearing in different guises — that's the heresy of modalism.

Rather, the doctrine is: *one God, three Persons.* These three Persons are equally God.

Consider this illustration. I once was an honorary assistant at St. Paul's Episcopal Church in Malden, Mass. St. Paul's had one clergy staff but three priests on the staff. There were not three separate staffs, but

---

[1]Catechism, *The Book of Common Prayer*, p. 852.

one staff. We were not one priest and two deacons, but three priests. The staff was not one priest appearing in three different guises, but three priests. One staff, three priests — one God, three Persons.

The word "Trinity" does not appear in the Bible. As with so many other doctrines, a later era of the Church searched the Scripture and pulled various passages together to make a theological statement that was logical, coherent, and true to God's revelation. Nevertheless, we clearly see the truths of the doctrine of the Trinity in Scripture.

One of the literary devices used in Scripture is *synonymous parallelism*, which means stating the same thing two or more times in a row using different words, or placing things of equal value in parallel with each other. When this happens, we know the author's intent is to tell us that the two (or more) thoughts in parallel are of equal importance, or essential parts of the whole. For example:

- "But you, beloved . . . pray in the Holy Spirit. Keep yourselves in God's love as you wait for the mercy of our Lord Jesus Christ . . . " (Jude 20-21)

- " . . . chosen according to the foreknowledge of God the Father, through the sanctifying work of the Spirit, for obedience to Jesus Christ . . . " (1 Peter 1:2)

- "The Spirit . . . the Spirit of God . . . the Spirit of Christ . . ." (Romans 8:9).

By placing the (Holy) Spirit in such a parallel sequence with the Father (sometimes referred to simply as God, other times as God the Father, other times as the Father) and the Son, it is obvious these three different writers of Scripture knew that the Holy Spirit is a member of the Godhead, equal in divinity with the Father and the Son. Then, of course, there's the obvious reference in Matthew 28:19: "baptizing them in the Name of the Father and of the Son and of the Holy Spirit."

Consider also this statement used in describing the spiritual gifts in 1 Corinthians 12:4-6. We see, in parallel, the phrases: "varieties of gifts, but the same Spirit," "varieties of service, but the same Lord" and "varieties of working, but it is the same God."

The repetition of the words "varieties of" shows us the words "gifts," "service," and "working" are three ways of saying the same thing. Therefore, when we see "Spirit," "Lord" and "God" (meaning "God the Father") in synonymous parallelism, we know they are of the same order and essence.

The first generation of Christians knew how different Jesus was from other teachers. We will look at this point more fully in the next chapter, but we can make a quick review of the evidence now. The accounts of our Lord's birth (Matthew 1:18-25; Luke 1:26-38; John 1:1-14) give clear evidence that the Gospel writers knew Jesus to be God.

More important, the Scripture writers recalled how Jesus *knew Himself* to be something other — how He knew and declared Himself to be God. How do we know this? First, Jesus took onto Himself the divine prerogative to forgive sin (Mark 2:5-11), a claim to divinity not lost on His audience. Second, He claimed to state the truth, not by quoting learned rabbis of previous generations, but *in His own name* (see His repeated "But I say unto you" statements). Third, He accepted Thomas' worship (John 20:28). Fourth, He placed Himself at the center of His message. Note the repeated *I am* statements, such as "I am the good shepherd" (John 10:11), "I am the resurrection and the life" (John 11:25) and "I am the way and the truth and the life" (John 14:6).

What all of this demonstrates is that the first generation of Christians knew what we now call the doctrine of the Trinity to be the truth, even though the Church did not spell out the doctrine until later.

What does the doctrine of the Trinity mean for us?

1. The Trinity illustrates the truth of 1 Corinthians 12 and 14, that the Church enjoys a variety of gifts but the same Lord.

The different Persons of the Trinity have different tasks in the work of salvation. The Son died on the Cross, not the Father or the Holy Spirit. The Holy Spirit was poured out on Pentecost, not the Father or the Son.

The persons of the Trinity do not work against each other in their respective tasks. In the garden, Jesus wanted the cup of the Cross to pass by His lips, but submitted to the Father's will. Jesus asked the Father to send the Spirit (John 14:16). The Spirit did not come to the Church on His own.

If there is diversity of ministry but unity of purpose in the Godhead, how can we in the Church do otherwise? Therefore, Christians can and should use their different gifts in ministry, but we must put aside our own agendas and egos and work together for the common good. There's no room for the attitude that "God told me to do this ministry and I submit to God alone and not to you, even if you are a leader."

2. The Trinity demonstrates order, obedience, and hierarchy.

God the Son is equal *in essence* to the Father — Jesus is just as much God as the Father is — but He is subordinate *in authority*. Jesus said He came to do His Father's will, not His own (John 4:34). Jesus referred to *essence* when He said "The Father and I are one" (John 10:30). Jesus referred to *authority* when He said "The Father is greater than I" (John 14:28).

Let me continue the illustration of three priests on one staff. While I was just as much a priest as the other two, I was subordinate in authority to the Rector.

He was the one in charge. To be sure, authority can be abused. If Church authorities ask us to believe or practice anything that is *clearly* unscriptural, our primary allegiance is to God, not Church authorities.

However, if the leadership of the Church is *not* asking us to believe unscriptural beliefs or practice or countenance unscriptural morality, it is our responsibility to submit to its leadership. Christianity is not a democracy. We have been placed under authority. While all Christians are equal in terms of worth before God, we are not equal in terms of our authority. Jesus Christ and the Holy Spirit, in submitting to God the Father, provide us the model of what life in the Church should be like.

3. **The different members of the Trinity illustrate different aspects of our relationship with the Godhead.**

The Father represents the transcendent dimension of God. We picture God the Father as mighty, exalted, enthroned in the heavenlies, overseeing the universe. He is, as the hymn puts it, "immortal, invisible, God only wise; in light inaccessible, hid from our eyes."

We picture God the Son as our Friend, our Brother, the One Who "walks with me and talks with me and tells me I am His own."

We picture God the Holy Spirit as the One Who comes to empower us for rapturous worship, holy living, and effective ministry, the One to whom we sing, "Come, Holy Spirit, heavenly Dove, with all Thy quickening powers."

When we focus too exclusively on one Person of the Trinity at the expense of the others, we will have a distorted understanding of God and a distorted spiritual life as well.

It seems that each of the three major streams of Christianity — Catholic, Protestant, Pentecostal — has embraced one member of the Trinity more than the other two. In doing so, each has captured the meaning and enjoyed the blessings of *that* Person of the Godhead better than other churches have, but to the partial neglect of the other two Persons.

Catholic Christians (Roman Catholics, Eastern Orthodox, Anglo-Catholic Episcopalians), focus on the transcendence of God the Father, best illustrated liturgically by the majesty of the High Mass, and architecturally by grand, awe-inspiring buildings. We respect God's holiness and authority. We are assured that God is, indeed, bigger than our problems or our foes.

Catholic Christianity, however, poses the danger of God disappearing into the vastness of the eternal heavens and becoming unapproachable. Some people pay excessive attention to saints because they are more keenly aware of God's *transcendence* (His being high, exalted) than of His *immanence* (His being here with us). God becomes virtually inaccessible for many Christians. In this setting, we remain dependent on ministry from the clergy, but do not receive God's power to minister in His name. And, while worship before this omnipotent, holy God is rich and beautiful, where is the focus on the study of His written word, Scripture?

Protestants focus much more — some would say exclusively — on Jesus. The hymn "What a Friend We Have in Jesus" celebrates His immanent presence right here with us. Knowing Him as our friend emphasizes the truths that He came to remove the separation between us and God caused by our sin, that He is The Teacher and we must focus on what He said, and that He is right here with us in a very approachable way.

The danger, of course, is that we can become overly familiar with Jesus in the wrong way — friendship can become flippant and irreverent. Jesus can easily become our "religious adviser" but not our sovereign Lord. Further, Protestants can become so focused on the *teaching* of Jesus that they see Christianity primarily as intellectual content, forgetting that God should be worshiped and adored. For example, in many Protestant churches, Sunday "worship" is primarily a sermon with a very few minutes devoted to song and prayer. Even this small amount is done in a "down here" style. One often needs to go to other kinds of churches to be enraptured in the Spirit or to be awed by God's majesty. Lest you think I am exaggerating, I have too often heard the music and prayers leading up to the sermon referred to as "the preliminaries."

Pentecostals and charismatics focus on the empowering work of the Holy Spirit for praise and for the ministry of all God's people. Pentecostals attempt to correct an often priest-centered Catholicism and an often mind-centered Protestantism. Pentecostal Christians want worship to be fervent and from the heart. Pentecostal Christians see ministry as more than acquiring professional skills and "being in a helping profession." Rather, Pentecostals understand that God equips all Christians through gifts of the Spirit to do the work of ministry.

A weakness of Pentecostal worship is that it sometimes focuses on good feelings more than on God. Some people judge a worship service not on whether it glorifies God, or teaches correct doctrine, or challenges worshipers to live in conformity to God's will, but on how good it made the worshiper feel. A second weakness is an anti-intellectualism that says we do not need to do the hard work of Scripture study since the Spirit can always give us a spontaneous "word." A third weakness is the notion that we do not have to be trained or supervised in ministry because empowerment by the Holy Spirit is sufficient.

I believe God wants us to be "full gospel Christians," enjoying the strengths of each of the three streams of Christianity — Catholic, Protestant, Pentecostal. Further, I believe that when we embrace all three of these streams, they serve as correctives to keep the weaknesses of each stream in check.

Let me ask you: While you may have a *correct doctrine* of the Trinity, do you have a *balanced walk* with the Trinity? While thanking God for what you know of Him, ask God to help you grow into a fuller appreciation of Him.

How do you do that? First, by asking God to make Himself known to you more fully and in ways different from what you have experienced.

Second, by reading spiritual books, trying devotional exercises, and attending worship services of a type different from what you are used to (and perhaps like best). For example, a charismatic should go to a solemn High Mass; one who likes simple worship focused primarily on teaching from Scripture should go to a praise service.

We should never, however, accept any teaching or experience just because it is different or seems "spiritual." As Scripture reminds us, we are to test doctrines to make sure they are from God (1 John 4:1). There are many expressions of spirituality, even in the Church, that are not in conformity with what God reveals in Scripture. We must reject them unless we believe ourselves wiser than God. However, the rich diversity of *orthodox* spiritual experiences broadens us as Christians. It helps us understand our fellow Christians whose expression of the faith is, while also orthodox, somewhat different. It gives us deeper knowledge of the Triune God.

DISCUSSION QUESTIONS:

1. Of the three streams of Christianity — Catholic, Protestant, and Pentecostal — which is the most familiar to you and which is the most foreign?

2. How is the unity-in-diversity of the Trinity an example for life in the Church?

3. How does referring to God "modally" (Creator/Redeemer/Sustainer) and not "personally" (Father/Son/Holy Spirit) erode the doctrine of the Trinity? What harm does this cause?

FOR FURTHER READING:

Kimel, Alvin, editor, *Speaking the Christian God*, William B. Eerdmans.

Lewis, C.S., "Beyond Personality: Or First Steps in the Doctrine of the Trinity," fourth section of *Mere Christianity*, Collier Books.

McGrath, Alister, *Understanding the Trinity*, Zondervan.

3

The Uniqueness
of Jesus Christ

Q. What do we mean when we say that Jesus is the only Son of God?
A. We mean that Jesus is the only perfect image of the Father, and shows us the nature of God.

Q. What do we mean when we say that Jesus was conceived by the power of the Holy Spirit and became incarnate from the Virgin Mary?
A. We mean that by God's own act, his divine Son received our human nature from the Virgin Mary, his mother.[1]

Jesus Christ is the center of the Christian faith. While most other religions center on observing duties or following ethical statements, Christianity centers in a person, Jesus Christ. Who Jesus is and what Jesus did on the Cross define Christianity.

Jesus knew His uniqueness as God-made-flesh, as God on earth in human form. He never came right out and said "I am God." If He had, some would have followed Him just for what they could get out of Him, and others would have immediately attempted to kill Him. No, Jesus had to convince people of His divinity in a real but less direct way. By doing this, the message would sink in deep, and would not lead either

---

[1]Catechism, *The Book of Common Prayer*, p. 849, sets 6 and 8.

to superficial discipleship or to His premature death. How do we know Jesus knew Himself to be the unique, divine Son of God, God the Second Person of the Trinity become a human being?

First, in His presumption to forgive sin, Jesus took upon Himself a prerogative of divinity. No Jewish leader, no matter how exalted, would dare make this claim. While the priestly leaders might assure people of God's forgiveness, they would never declare that forgiveness as if they were God doing it in person. Jesus did, and His audience did not miss His point (see Mark 2:5-12).

Second, in the way Jesus referred to God, Jesus indicated He was God's Son in a unique way. The Jews caught that point and sought to put Him to death as a blasphemer because, John tells us, the Jews believed that Jesus made Himself equal with God (John 5:18).

Some people today naively say Jesus never claimed equality with God. Although not agreeing with His claim, Jesus' opponents at least accurately understood the claim He made. They knew what He was saying!

Third, in the way Jesus spoke of Himself. Even a casual reading of the Gospels demonstrates that Jesus put Himself at the center of His message. Consider Jesus' various "I am" statements (see, for example, John 6:35, 15:1); the way Jesus pointed out that to know Him was to know God the Father (John 14:9); the way Jesus made Himself the key to eternal life (John 14:6); and the way He accepted the worship of Thomas (John 20:26-29).

He Who counseled humility in others made extraordinary statements about Himself. As many have noted, in making such egocentric statements, Jesus was either a lunatic, or He was a liar trying to flimflam people, or He was exactly what He claimed to be. One thing is certain. He was not just "a good teacher." What good teacher places Himself at the center of His message? To the person who insists on calling Jesus "a good teacher," I would issue this challenge: *if He's such a good teacher, then believe His message,* which includes teachings about the resurrection and all the statements about Who He is.

Along with reporting Jesus' taking divine prerogatives to Himself and quoting His claims about Himself, the Scripture writers themselves assert our Lord's divinity. By spending time with Him and listening to Him teach, and by divine revelation, they knew our Lord's divinity. The writer of the Epistle to the Hebrews starts His book in this way:

> In the past God spoke to our forefathers through the prophets at many times and in various ways, but in these last days he has spoken to us by his Son, whom he appointed heir of all things, and through whom he made the universe.[2]

John describes the Word (logos) as being God, and writes that this Word became flesh as Jesus of Nazareth (John 1:1, 14-18). While we can become *adopted* children of God by belief in Jesus Christ (John 1:12), Jesus is the Son of God by His very nature and from all eternity.

So what? What difference does it make that the second Person of the Godhead came to earth as Jesus of Nazareth and that this Jesus is the unique incarnation of God in the flesh?

First, with God coming to earth personally, we have ultimate truth spoken directly to us in human language. We have trustworthy answers to the various questions that vex our minds. Why, then, settle for anything less? Jesus said it Himself: The truth sets us free (John 8:32).

People often come up with new theologies that deny the truth of what Scripture teaches. They think these new theologies liberate, but they never do. These new theologies — announced with so much fanfare and usually with a smirk directed at those who believe orthodox Biblical teaching — quickly become outdated, replaced by the next wave of new theologies. We may need humility to set aside our cherished pet innovative doctrines and alternative moralities and submit to what Scripture says, but it is the path not only of discipleship, but also of wisdom.

Because He is God, Jesus is sovereign Lord. To believe in Jesus is to believe everything He said. Jesus' earthly ministry came at a time of great controversy within Judaism. The Pharisees, Sadducees, Zealots, Essenes, and doubtless other factions disagreed heatedly over a whole

---

[2]Hebrews 1:1-2, NIV.

variety of matters. Into the midst of this Jesus came, not to effect compromise, nor to offer His "own opinions, for whatever they're worth," nor to minimize the importance of discovering the truth, but to give the final, authoritative answer on matters of doctrine and morals.

Look, for example, at His discussion with some Sadducees about the resurrection. Jesus did not tell them He had a different opinion, but that they were wrong (Mark 12:24). On morality, Jesus took what was contemporary Jewish practice and toughened the demands. (See, for example, the various "You have heard that it was said, but I say to you" statements in Matthew 5:21-2, 27-8, 31-2, 33-4.)

In a conversation with His closest friends in the Upper Room, Jesus reminded them what following Him entailed. In telling them that He is Truth (John 14:6), and that if they love Him they will keep His commandments (John 14:15), Jesus makes clear what discipleship means: Submission of one's mind and heart to Him, and a Spirit-filled ministry to others with the expectation that lives will be transformed and miracles will happen.

Therefore, when orthodox Christians insist that the Church believes the doctrines and practices the morality that Christ taught, they are not being arrogant or narrow-minded. They are being faithful to Christ. Evangelism that lacks this fidelity is not evangelism but mere membership recruitment. Jesus reiterates this point in His Great Commission statement in Matthew 28:19-20: "Therefore go and make *disciples* of all nations . . . *teaching them to obey everything I have commanded you*" (italics added). To the souls weary of our culture's hedonism, the stale bread and poisoned water of theological liberalism fails to satisfy.

Had Christ come as just one of many incarnations or manifestations of God, we would bumble along in confusion. As the founders of the various religions of the world disagree on so many basic things, who is right? (Only the most superficial understanding of world religions would conclude that "all religions teach the same thing." Anyone who has studied them knows the world's religions differ significantly on basic matters.)

Jesus presumed to correct the misunderstandings or partial understandings of the various Jewish groups of His day. Likewise, He presumes to correct the misunderstandings or partial understandings of other teachers, gurus and religious leaders of today. When we submit to Jesus' teaching, faithfully recorded in Scripture, we are set free from subjectivity and bondage to our own misunderstandings.

Second, with God coming to earth personally, we have a great high priest Who sympathizes with our weaknesses (Hebrews 4:15). When we pray, we know that our friend Jesus walked the same roads we walk and suffered the same hurts, problems, privations and temptations we suffer, and that this Jesus now sits at the right hand of God the Father to make intercession for us (Hebrews 7:25-8).

The Uniqueness of the Atonement

Q. What is the great importance of Jesus' suffering and death?
A. By his obedience, even to suffering and death, Jesus made the offering which we could not make; in him we are freed from the power of sin and reconciled to God.[3]

Jesus came to die in our place to atone for our sins — sinless Redeemer for sinful people — so that those who trust in Him can have eternal life (Mark 10:45, John 3:16). Jesus never spoke of His crucifixion as *inevitable* ("that's what happens when you buck the establishment") but as *necessary*, as God's way to redeem us. The Father would not let this cup pass by His Son because it was only through Christ bearing our sins that we could be freed from their penalty (Matthew 26:39).

As the writer of the Epistle to the Hebrews put it, "he entered the Most Holy Place once for all by his own blood, having obtained eternal redemption" (9:12). As Paul put it, "For the wages of sin is death, but the (free) gift of God is eternal life in Christ Jesus our Lord" (Romans 6:23).

This truth of the atoning work of Jesus Christ was the basic organizing principle of the Eucharistic Prayer in *The Book of Common Prayer*. For Thomas Cranmer, author of the first *Book of Common Prayer*, Christ's "ransom for many" (Mark 10:45) was the key to it all. His words, which live today in Rite I of *The Book of Common Prayer*, are so incisive:

---

[3]Catechism, *The Book of Common Prayer*, p. 850, set 2.

"by his one oblation of himself once offered, [he made] a full, perfect, and sufficient sacrifice, oblation, and satisfaction for the sins of the whole world" (page 334).

Why should this matter so much? Why should our voices cry out loudly in protest against the denial of this truth?

First, because Christ's atoning work — the innocent Saviour paying the penalty price for our sins to save us — is *the heart of the Gospel*. To deny this most basic truth is to take away the Good News and substitute "another Gospel." If our Lord and the writers of the Epistles are wrong on this most important topic, about what else are they mistaken? If we cannot have confidence in God's written word, which the Psalmist calls "a lamp to my feet and a light to my path," we are back in the dark (Psalm 119:105).

We have to be extremely vigilant that those issuing new or rewording existing liturgies and hymnals are not using occasions of revision to alter either the basic Gospel message or God's description of Himself, both of which were given to us by God conclusively in Scripture.

Second, this point is crucial because the alternatives to the Gospel are not messages of good news. While the message of Jesus brings rescue, these so-called new revelations from God are false and bring bondage. Let's look at a few of these "alternative" messages:

One alternative to the biblical message is to deny sin. In other words, people may choose to do whatever they wish and our job as the Church is not to tell them they are wrong — that might hurt their self-esteem — but to affirm them in their choices, beliefs, or life-styles, whatever they are.

What's wrong with this? First, that's not at all what Christ did. While affirming *people*, our Lord roundly and regularly condemned wrong *behavior*. He still does!

Second, given free reign, without submitting to the Lord's truth, people inevitably choose wrongly. Left to our own devices, we are ignorant of what is good and right. Without the empowerment of the Holy Spirit, we are unable to fulfill our desires to improve. We need Scripture to tell us.

Do we really believe that people, apart from God's revelation and grace, will choose what is right and do it? Do we really believe that all people need is some education and they will be fine? Look at the scandals that break out regularly, often featuring the cultured and educated as much as anyone else. At the turn of the century, some believed the human race had come of age, and no longer needed the restraints of Scripture or the law. Can we honestly say the wars and holocausts of the 20th century have demonstrated we have come of age?

Third, what God has declared to be right and just is also what is best for us. Doctors now tell us that monogamy significantly lowers the risk of contracting many diseases such as cervical cancer. To teach a "morality" that contradicts Scripture may sound liberal and inclusive. The truth is, such training leads people to rebel against God and may set people up for any number of diseases. Simply put, theological liberalism does not liberate.

A second alternative to the biblical message is to say God exacts no punishment for sin. Because He is a God of love, so this argument goes, He may try to influence us, but the notion of punishment belongs back in the Dark Ages.

This reduces God either to a permissive parent raising a brood of spoiled little brats or a whining parent, always saying "please don't" but never doing anything about it when we sin. Our sense of justice cries out instinctively when a rapist or a child molester goes free with a slap on the wrist, or when a country refuses to impose sanctions on a foreign government that practices apartheid or genocide. If God does not hold people accountable, and if there is no punishment from on high, the racists in South Africa have nothing of ultimate significance to worry about, and Adolf Hitler went from his suicide bunker directly to heavenly bliss. If God does not hold people accountable, how dare we?

25

We know that when there is no punishment from lawfully constituted authorities, vigilante justice quickly arises, and it usually is not good. When we read, "'It is mine to avenge; I will repay,' says the Lord" (Leviticus 19:18, quoted in Romans 12:19 and Hebrews 10:30), we have the assurance that God ordered the universe according to what is right and just, and that there will be a final day of reckoning, and that human government and Church authorities, while imperfect, are not wrong to regulate behavior and punish disobedience.

> Q. What do we mean by the last judgment?
> A. We believe that Christ will come in glory and judge the living and the dead.[4]

A third alternative to the biblical message is that God grades on the curve, punishing only the most heinous crimes and sins.

This raises another question: Where does one draw the line? If the only alternatives are jaywalking and mass murder, drawing the line would not be difficult; but with billions of people on planet Earth, the gradations between levels of sin become exceedingly fine. Exactly where is it on the scale that the heavier punishments kick in? If this is how God judges, why did Jesus not say so? Actually, He ruled it out: "Be perfect, therefore, as your heavenly Father is perfect" (Matthew 5:48).

Wise and true is the insight of those holy people who recognize the depth and perniciousness of sin still within themselves. Rather than argue that their sins are not as bad as those of others, the truly virtuous fall on their knees before the Lord saying, "Have mercy on me a sinner" (Luke 18:13).

A fourth alternative to the Biblical message is the belief that we can earn our way to heaven. This is "man in the street" religion. Sadly, it is the belief of many in the Church, even though everything in our liturgy, hymnal, and Scripture readings is diametrically opposite.

There are a couple of variations on this theme. One is that if we do enough good deeds we balance out the bad deeds and can, therefore, earn our way to heaven. In reality, however, we are not nearly as virtuous

---

[4]Ibid., p. 862, set 4.

as we believe. We claim to be generous, but how much do we give away? We boast that we have never committed adultery, but Jesus said that if we have ever looked with lust on someone we have committed adultery in our hearts (Matthew 5:28). Can we say we've never done that? The fact is, our virtue is not very deep, and sin always seems to pop up when we thought we had the problem licked. Further, when we do something virtuous, doesn't pride raise its head?

Remember the words of the Prayer of Humble Access: "We do not presume to come to this Thy table, trusting in our own righteousness." This statement is not religious neurosis, but is true to the Gospel and reflective of the heart attitude of the truly holy person. It is instructive for the rest of us. If we could earn our salvation, we are saying that Jesus' coming to earth as Saviour was unnecessary, that somehow God made a big mistake in sending His Son to save those who could save themselves. Jesus' belief that He came to save sinners was somehow mistaken if they can save themselves.

A variation on the theme that we can earn our salvation is the belief that, through reincarnation, we can come back to make atonement for our misdeeds by suffering in this life and in future lives. Belief in reincarnation and in *karma* — literally, "the result of one's deeds" — are catching on in America today. It sounds fair. After all, why should someone else, like Jesus, suffer for what I do wrong?

If bearing our own karmic debt is the way to deal with the problem of sin and justice, then what does this say for society? We need not postulate theories but only look at those countries where beliefs in reincarnation and *karma* are widely accepted — India, for example. Where do the hospitals and clinics come from if not from Christian missionaries or secularized or converted native citizens? If *karma* is true and you come across people lying in a ditch suffering, what you should do is *leave them there*. Why? If you help them you are interfering with their paying off karmic debt. Your help will only set them back, perhaps condemning them to suffer even more in this or future lives. As with every other false belief, belief in reincarnation has destructive ramifications for individuals and for society.

All these alternative views, these spiritual counterfeits, follow from a refusal to honor Jesus Christ as the unique Son of God, the only Lord and Saviour, and the authoritative Teacher of truth.

Jesus knew that the truth sets us free (John 8:32). In the short haul, denial of God's truth in society or in the Church may not make a significant difference as a few generations will live in the twilight's afterglow and believe and behave in a semi-Christian manner. But eventually the darkness sets in as people live in the bondage to which non-truth always leads. Because personal trust in the atoning work of Christ on the Cross is the *only* way an individual can be saved for eternity, there are eternal consequences for rejecting the Christ of Scripture for a way of salvation of our own design.

For those who have put their trust in Jesus Christ as Lord and Saviour, there is Godly counsel now and eternal life later. "But thanks be to God! He gives us the victory through our Lord Jesus Christ" (1 Corinthians 15:57).

DISCUSSION QUESTIONS:

1. What difference does it make that Jesus Christ is God?

2. What difference does it make that Jesus Christ went to the Cross?

3. Discuss the saying "It is hard to believe because it is hard to obey."

FOR FURTHER READING:

Lewis, C.S., *The Weight of Glory*, Macmillan Publishing.

Stott, John R.W., *The Cross of Christ*, InterVarsity Press.

4

The Holy Spirit

The Holy Spirit has been called "the forgotten Person of the Trinity." Many Christians find it easy to speak of God the Father. Many Christians know the Lord Jesus Christ. Fewer Christians know very much about the Holy Spirit, despite the various movements of renewal in the Church. Many Christians refer to the Holy Spirit as *it* rather than *He*, or speak of *what* rather than *Who* the Holy Spirit is.

> Q. Who is the Holy Spirit?
> A. The Holy Spirit is the Third Person of the Trinity, God at work in the world and in the Church even now.[1]

Throughout the centuries, the Church has acknowledged the Holy Spirit to be one of the Persons of the Trinity. In short, the Holy Spirit is God. There are not many statements about the divinity of the Holy Spirit in Scripture. When they do occur, like those statements about the divinity of Jesus, they are indirect. The Scriptures spend more time on what the Holy Spirit wishes to do in the lives of believers to transform us into maturity and empower us to engage in ministry.

The Holy Spirit does many things in the world and in the Church. Among His various ministries:

1. The Holy Spirit will glorify Jesus and continue His work to God's

---

[1]Catechism, *The Book of Common Prayer*, p. 852, set 5.

people. Jesus, although equal with God the Father in divine essence, submitted to the Father's will. Likewise, the Holy Spirit, although equal with the Father and the Son in divine essence, glorifies Jesus (John 16:14). Just as Jesus is Truth (John 14:6), the Spirit is "the Spirit of Truth" (John 14:17). Just as Jesus' ministry was to speak to the world about sin and salvation, so too will the Spirit come to convince the world of these things (John 16:8-11).

The Holy Spirit is another *paraklete* to be with the Church once the Lord has ascended back to heaven (John 14:16). That word *paraklete*, often translated Counselor or Comforter, comes from two Greek words — *para*, which means "alongside of" or "with," and *kalein*, which means "to call." Thus, the Holy Spirit is the one Who comes to us, calling to us with words of strength and words of comfort, continuing what Jesus did when He was on earth.

2. The Holy Spirit inspires the words of Scripture and guarantees their accuracy.

> Q. How do we recognize the truths taught by the Holy Spirit?
> A. We recognize truths to be taught by the Holy Spirit when they are in accord with the Scriptures.[2]

We know from the Gospels what great store Jesus put in the truth, which is what sets us free (John 8:32). Not surprisingly, therefore, Jesus made provision for His words of truth to be remembered and written down for subsequent generations. It would make no sense for Jesus to come to correct our thinking and our behaving if His words were heard by but one generation while garbled for subsequent generations. Additionally, God's revelation was still to be completed through the authors of the Epistles, and this too needed to be heard and recorded accurately: "But the Counselor, the Holy Spirit, whom the Father will send in my name, will teach you all things and will remind you of everything I have said to you" (John 14:26, John 16:12-13).

As 2 Timothy 3:16 reminds us, Scripture is *inspired*. We should understand that the word inspired in Scripture means more than just

---

[2]Ibid., p. 853, first set

"creative," as in the statement "Shakespeare was an inspired writer." In Greek, the word for "inspired" means, literally, God-breathed.

Jesus' statement that the Spirit will lead them into all truth does not mean that the Holy Spirit continues to give fresh doctrinal or ethical revelation today. When Jesus says the Holy Spirit will lead "you" into all truth, it is the same "you" to whom He has just said "I have spoken to you, while I am still with you." Jesus was speaking of the revelation given to the writers of the Acts of the Apostles, the Epistles and the book of Revelation, those comprising the generation of the Apostles.

Subsequent generations of early Church leaders made no such assertion about the Holy Spirit giving them fresh doctrinal or ethical revelations, nor should we today. When it comes to hearing new revelations that separate us from Scriptural revelation — given unchangeably once and for all — Jesus made no such promise and held no such expectation.

As the Catechism points out, the Scriptures stand over any purported revelations "given by the Spirit" today, and not the other way around.

3. The Holy Spirit seeks to work "sanctification" in Christian believers to make us more like Jesus.

Q. How is the Holy Spirit revealed in the New Covenant?
A. The Holy Spirit is revealed as the Lord who . . . enables us to grow in the likeness of Christ.[3]

We are called to be "imitators of God" (Ephesians 5:1). What is a Godly person like? According to Scripture, a Godly person has abundant Fruits of the Spirit: love, joy, peace, patience, kindness, goodness, faithfulness, gentleness, and self-control (Galatians 5:22-3).

How do we get to be like that? The phrase "Fruit of the Spirit" gives us the answer. These traits are not anything we can produce ourselves. We cannot decide or will to be more gentle. Becoming authentically more gentle is the work of the Holy Spirit within us. This does not mean we have nothing to do in the process of sanctification. Our job is to be constant

---

[3]Ibid., p. 852, seventh set

and disciplined in the duties of the faith — worship, Scripture reading, prayer, faithful reception of Holy Communion, ministering to and receiving ministry from other Christians, and calling upon the assistance of God and others when we are tempted to sin. Not to do these things is to grieve the Holy Spirit (Ephesians 4:30), because He so wants to make us Godly.

To use an agricultural analogy, we cannot produce tomatoes on a plant, but we must put in the tomato plant, and water, cultivate, and fertilize it. While only God can grow a tomato, God expects us to do the farming. We are wrong to think we can make tomatoes occur. We are also wrong to leave it all up to God.

4. The Holy Spirit wishes to manifest various "spiritual gifts" to help us in our work for God. In the Upper Room Jesus told His closest friends that they would have the same type of miraculous ministry as He Himself had (John 14:12). After they were empowered by the Holy Spirit on the Day of Pentecost (Acts 2), the disciples experienced exactly that.

God placed no time limit on the manifestation of the spiritual gifts. We should expect them to occur in the Church today, just as they have throughout the centuries. We need to note several popular, but erroneous, attitudes people have concerning the spiritual gifts:

The first erroneous attitude is, *it's wrong to ask for them*. Sometimes people come to that conclusion because they see individuals misusing the spiritual gifts God has given them. Gifts are not *trophies* proving how wonderful we are, or *toys* to play with, but *tools* needed for service in the Kingdom.

A man once asked me if he should be concerned with the spiritual gifts. I asked what he did for a living. He told me he was a carpenter. I asked if he should be concerned with saws, hammers, and planes. "Of course," he said. "These are my tools. I need them to do my work." He got the point! Asking God for spiritual gifts is wise if we are asking Him to equip us to serve better. Asking for spiritual gifts is not wrong if we want them to enable or enhance our glorifying Him and serving others. Scripture tells us to strive for the spiritual gifts (1 Corinthians 14:1).

The second erroneous attitude is, *it's wrong to acknowledge having spiritual gifts, since that would be boastful.* Since Scripture says each believer has one or more spiritual gifts (1 Corinthians 12:7), to say you do not have a gift is to say Scripture is wrong. It is a false humility, or perhaps an evasion of responsibility. Besides, how will you know to what ministry God is likely calling you, or how will you take the effort to hone your ministry gifts, if you do not acknowledge what your gifts are? It is boasting only if you call undue attention to your gifts or take credit for the blessings that occur through your ministry.

The third erroneous attitude is, *the spiritual gifts are okay for the charismatics but since I'm not a charismatic I need not be concerned with them.* We need to make a careful distinction between the gifts of the Holy Spirit and the cultural trappings often associated with the charismatic movement. It is easy to be confused, since many of us have seen the spiritual gifts at work only in settings distinctly "charismatic" in style. A careful reading of Church history will show that the spiritual gifts have been in operation throughout the centuries and in Church settings that look very different in their trappings. I have seen various spiritual gifts manifested in the midst of Solemn High Mass with lots of incense; in quiet, simple Protestant worship services; and in formal, traditional, "middle of the road" Episcopal settings. The external trappings of the charismatic subculture — informality, free-form liturgy, contemporary music, guitars — are optional. What's not optional is our active ministry in the power of the Holy Spirit, using whatever spiritual gifts God has chosen to give us.

The fourth erroneous attitude is, *since the Holy Spirit gives us gifts for ministry, I can just let the Spirit work through me. For me to study, take courses, or even be supervised by others would block the Holy Spirit's work.*

We need special balance on this issue. Paul told His young protege Timothy to stir up the gift that was within Him (2 Timothy 1:6). Paul also told Timothy to work at honing it for service (2 Timothy 2:15). Paul's guidance of Timothy should speak to us who wish to serve God. It's not either/or — either the empowerment of the Spirit or study/training/supervision — it's both/and.

The fifth erroneous attitude is, *once the Holy Spirit gives me a gift, that's my gift for life*. The gift is never *ours*, but God's gift on loan to us, used for the common good of His people, under the supervision of the leaders He has placed over us. The most humble statement a person can make is to say a talent is "on loan from God." God has every right to use us in one particular ministry for a time and then change the focus. While those who flit from ministry to ministry every few months are exhibiting signs of spiritual immaturity, it is not uncommon for people to be moved, on occasion, to another type of spiritual giftedness and to another area of service.

The sixth erroneous attitude is, *for something to be a spiritual gift it has to be spectacular and unlike anything I know how to do*. Wrong on both counts! While some gifts *are* spectacular (like prophecy or working miracles), other gifts (like administration or giving help) are rather quiet. While God sometimes gives us the ability, when ministering under the empowerment of the Holy Spirit, to do something totally unlike anything we've ever studied or different from what we are like apart from His empowerment, sometimes God takes an ability we have had for some time and, as it were, "supernaturalizes" it for a deeper, more effective use.[4]

DISCUSSION QUESTIONS:

1. Of the spiritual gifts listed in Scripture (see Romans 12:6-8, 1 Corinthians 12 and 14, Ephesians 4:4-16), which gifts do you think God has given you?

2. Why do many Church members pull back from the person and activities of the Holy Spirit?

3. We know the spiritual gifts can be misused. What can we do to make sure they are used wisely so we neither get burned by their misuse nor overreact and turn our backs on the Spirit's activity?

---

[4]If you would like to look at the various spiritual gifts in further detail, read Romans 12:6-8, 1 Corinthians 12 an 14, and Ephesians 4:4-16.

FOR FURTHER READING:

Bennett, Dennis, *Nine O'clock in the Morning*, Bridge Publishing.

Green, Michael, *I Believe in the Holy Spirit*, Eerdmans.

Lovelace, Richard, *Dynamics of Spiritual Life*, InterVarsity Press.

McDonnell, Kilian, and George T. Montague, *Christian Initiation and Baptism in the Holy Spirit*, The Liturgical Press.

Pearson, Mark A., *Christian Healing*, Chosen Books.

Pytches, David, *Spiritual Gifts in the Local Church*, Bethany House Publishers.

5

The Bible

Q. Why do we call the Holy Scriptures the Word of God?
A. We call them the Word of God because God inspired their human authors and because God still speaks to us through the Bible.[1]

When people come either to a new or deeper relationship with Jesus Christ, the Bible takes on a new importance. They discover their friend Jesus in its pages, they find sage advice for daily living, and they find, as Princeton Seminary professor Emile Cailliet once said, "a book that understands me."

But the question quickly arises, should we deem the Bible the authoritative Word of God? The answer is an overwhelming yes, and for several reasons.

First is the example of our Lord Jesus Christ. He trusted Scripture and commanded us to do the same. As we read the Gospels we discover Jesus trusted in the authority of the Old Testament as God's Word. He did this in three ways:

- By doing things "that the Scriptures might be fulfilled" (see Mark 14:49; Luke 24:44-45; John 17:12, 19:28);

- By repeatedly using phrases such as "it is written" and "have you not read?" (see Matthew 19:4, 21:13; Mark 2:25, 9:12);

---

[1]Catechism, *The Book of Common Prayer*, p. 853, set 6.

- By challenging the Pharisees who added to Scripture their personal customs and traditions, which nullified the teachings of the Old Testament (see Matthew 15:3, 23:23), and by challenging the Sadducees, who subtracted teachings from it (Matthew 22:23-33).

In addition, Jesus prepared for a New Testament with similar authority:

- By saying that the Holy Spirit would jog the minds of the Gospel writers so they would be accurate in what they wrote (John 14:26);

- By saying that those writing the Epistles would transmit God's revelation, not their own opinions (John 16:12-13).

Trusting the Bible as the authoritative Word of God is what Jesus did and would have us do.

The second reason is the practice of the historic Church. Early Church leaders wrote letters to other churches to strengthen their faith and correct doctrinal and moral errors. They cited Scripture as the authority for what they said.

While not shirking in their own personal authority as Church leaders, they did not place their own opinions or writings on a par with Scripture. Even in its early centuries, the Church considered the Old and New Testaments significantly different from the thoughts and writings of others.

The Anglican Communion, of which the Episcopal Church is a part, has taken a similar approach throughout the centuries. Read the Articles of Religion, especially articles 6, 8, 20 and 34 (*The Book of Common Prayer*, pages 867-876), to see how central Scripture is in Anglican belief. While Anglicans consider many beliefs and customs optional or negotiable, Scriptural authority is not optional. The Chicago-Lambeth Quadrilateral clearly refers to the Holy Scriptures as "the revealed Word of God." The Lambeth Conference of 1888 calls Holy Scriptures "the rule and ultimate standard of faith." (See *The Book of Common Prayer*, pages 876-77.) The great Anglican leader Richard Hooker (1554-1600), while noting the authority of Scripture, tradition and reason, clearly placed Scripture as primary over the other two. He wrote: "What Scripture doth plainly deliver it is that the *first* place of both credit and obedience is due" (*Ecclesiastical Polity*, Book V, Chapter 8, Section II).

The Church has recognized Scripture as the authoritative voice of God. This doesn't mean the Church bestows this authority on the Bible. That would mean the Church, not Scripture, is the ultimate authority in belief and conduct. Rather, the Church recognizes the ultimate authority *inherent* in Scripture, and *bows* before that authority. As the Lambeth Conference of 1968 said: "The Church is not over the Holy Scriptures, but under them.... To that apostolic authority the Church must ever bow."[2]

The third reason for believing in the authority of Scripture is that Scripture is self-authenticating. We find in daily life that what the Bible says is true in human experience. Much as we would like to dismiss the Bible's doctrinal or moral teaching as nonsense, eventually we discover that what it says squares with the way things really are.

The difficulties many people have with the Bible are *moral* and not *intellectual*, for some of the greatest minds throughout the centuries have been orthodox, Biblical Christians. It isn't that some intelligent people *cannot* believe what the Bible says. Instead, it's that many people, whatever their intelligence, *will not* believe what the Bible says, because such belief demands changes in behavior and attitude.

If you are not sure that the Bible is the trustworthy Word of God, the final arbiter for all questions of faith and morals, I encourage you to read the Bible intensively, asking the Holy Spirit to guide you in your search. If you read Scripture with an open mind, I believe you will see that, as Jesus taught, this is the Word of the Lord.

How should we study the Bible?

---

[2]The Lambeth Conferences is a gathering of Anglican bishops from around the world that usually occurs every decade. While its decisions are not binding, they do represent the mind of the worldwide Anglican Communion leaders on given subjects.

Prayerfully. Since we discern spiritual truths only in spiritual ways (see 1 Corinthians 2:13-14), we must seek God's help in studying Scripture. Not only does this mean we should begin and close our time of Bible study with prayer for divine illumination; we also must be in a prayerful attitude throughout our study. We humbly let God teach us from His word, refusing to impose our own pet doctrines and prejudices onto the text.

Faithfully. We have already seen Jesus' attitude to the Scriptures. Since "a disciple is not above His master" (Luke 6:40), the attitude of our Lord to the Scriptures must be ours as well. We should read the Bible, then, not as human gropings towards an unknown God, but as God's revelation of heavenly truths through the words of His servants. Pray also for the humility to adjust your opinions and actions accordingly.

Expectantly. Approach your time of Bible reading with anticipation, expecting the God Who took the time to communicate with humanity to help us see how that message applies to daily living. The writers of Scripture themselves remind us how relevant Scripture is:

- "All Scripture is God-breathed and is useful for teaching, rebuking, correcting and training in righteousness, so that the man of God may be thoroughly equipped for every good work" (2 Timothy 3:16-17).

- "How can a young man keep his way pure? By living according to your word" (Psalm 119:9).

- ". . . so that through endurance and the encouragement of the Scriptures we might have hope" (Romans 15:4).

Systematically. Too often we reduce Bible study to grabbing a few verses here and there, or only when we feel like it. Neither approach yields much fruit. Rather, set aside a specific time each day to study a regular amount of Scripture. Prayerfully and thoughtfully considering 15 verses each day is more profitable than grabbing a verse on the run or spending two hours in study followed by days of nothing. Determine how much you can expect to do each day and discipline yourself to do it.

Intelligently. Two enemies of Bible study are the arrogant exaltation of our minds on the one hand and a mindless anti-intellectualism on the other. God chose to reveal Himself in ways that call on our reason.

We must strike an important balance when considering Scripture to be God's truths written in human form. While acknowledging Scripture to be the truth, some fundamentalists seriously underplay the role of human authors. Some Christians build doctrines on verses taken out of context, or they make unwarranted inferences on the words of an outmoded translation.

Liberals, while appreciating the role of human authorship, do not acknowledge that God is the ultimate author of Scripture, guaranteeing faithful transmission of His message. Liberals see the Bible as a record of the religious insights and experiences of ancient cultures, perhaps interesting, perhaps misleading, but not authoritative for today.

The truth is, Scripture is the written Word of God expressed in the various styles of human authors.

Jesus told us to love God with our minds (Matthew 22:37). This means humbling our minds before sacred Scripture and using scholar's tools to understand what God is telling us. These tools include:

A concordance. This is a list of all (or, in the case of an abridged concordance, the more important) times Scripture uses a given word. It is dishonest and misleading to grab a verse that speaks to one aspect of the subject while ignoring other verses that speak to the rest of it. Do you want to see what God is saying about healing? Using a concordance, look up every reference for heal, heals, healed and healing and read these verses carefully.

A Bible atlas. Instead of just wondering where Beor is, look it up on a map.

A Bible dictionary. This is an alphabetically arranged series of topical presentations on given subjects. Are you interested in a topic like "angels"? A Bible dictionary will give you a thorough presentation of the subject, citing relevant Scriptural texts. Bible dictionaries often include a small listing of books and articles addressing the subject in greater detail.

Commentaries. A commentary is a verse-by-verse discussion of a book of the Bible. Commentaries exist at various levels of difficulty and for various purposes. Devotional commentaries discuss the scriptural text to promote better personal discipleship in the reader. Study commentaries look at the text primarily to define technical words, to set the passage in a historical context, and to compare and contrast the passage with other Scriptures. Often a commentary will do both. Just make sure the purpose of the commentary's author is to exalt the truths of Scripture, not to tear them down or explain them away.

Inquiringly. Ask several questions of the passage as you are reading it.

What does it tell me about God? Since God is infinite and holy, we can know little of God except what He reveals of Himself. Many people have some rather curious beliefs about Who God is. Through Scripture, we can get the real story directly from God.

What does it tell me about people? Some people believe humans are nothing more than the current end-product of an evolutionary process produced by impersonal time plus chance. Such a human being can be aborted, slaughtered or euthanized. Others believe that humans are godlike, able to build a glorious civilization without reference to God. Still others believe that human beings are part of God, able to master at least part of the universe. The Bible, however, supports neither the debasing nor the deification of humans. In Scripture, we learn about who we are from the God Who made us.

What does it tell me about salvation? Anthropologists tell us that almost every religion teaches that humans are estranged from God and need salvation. Beliefs about how to achieve this salvation differ markedly from one religion to the next. As you read Scripture, notice carefully what God says about our need for salvation and how this should occur.

What does it tell me to do? In Scripture God gives us some directives on how to live a holy life — both in specific do's and don'ts and in broad principles. If Jesus is truly the Lord of our life, we will want to please Him by obeying Him (John 14:15).

What does it warn me to avoid? The Old Testament records the words of God's prophets calling people to repent of various sins. In the Gospels we read various statements made by Jesus about what constitutes sin and righteousness. Most of the Epistles warn people off false doctrine and false behavior. Since the Epistles are equally the word of the Lord, we must take their warning against heresy and immorality as God's message to us. We cannot set these warnings aside merely because they are not the direct words of Jesus.

What does it promise me? Our lives can be enriched considerably when we realize that God has many blessings for us today. While we hear in the Communion service a general statement about "innumerable benefits procured unto us" (*The Book of Common Prayer*, p. 335), in Scripture we learn about the specific benefits.

What answers does it have for my personal questions? We all have questions about the ultimate issues of life. We also have particular questions that are perhaps important only to us. Keep these questions in mind as you read Scripture. You will be amazed how often you find passages that supply answers and guidance.

Communally. As the Catechism expresses it, "We understand the meaning of the Bible by the help of the Holy Spirit, who guides the Church in the true interpretation of the Scriptures."[3]

One of the most common mistakes people make when studying Scripture is to cling tenaciously to personal interpretation of a passage. Whether we study the Bible individually or in a group, we should compare our conclusions with the understandings of the wider Christian community, both today and throughout the centuries.

Most cults begin by a religious leader presuming to have some new insight or presuming to have the key to the Scriptures no one else has.

---

[3]Ibid., p. 853, last set.

Most heresies begin by a Church leader doing the same. Rather, test your insights and compare your conclusions by discovering what mature Christian Bible students believe. Read contemporary Christian writers and anointed teachers of the past.

In short, remember the Apostle Peter's statement that "no prophecy of Scripture came about by the prophet's own interpretation" (2 Peter 1:20). Also remember the Scriptural injunction, "Do not be wise in your own eyes" (Proverbs 3:7).

Purposefully. Close your time of study with prayer and a renewed commitment to God. Determine with His help to practice what Scripture commands you to do (see James 1:22). Ask God to fulfill His promises in your own life, in His way and in His time. Pray that the Holy Spirit will correct any of your erroneous interpretations as you compare them with the historic faith of the Church. Desire that your reading of Scripture will lead you to closer personal fellowship with God (see John 5:39). Take away with you at least one thought for the day on which to reflect — a promise to claim, a sin to renounce, a command to obey, a hope to cherish, a truth to ponder, a spiritual intimacy to celebrate.

With careful, determined Scripture study a regular part of your life, you can say with the Psalmist, "Thy Word is a lamp to my feet and a light to my path" (Psalm 119:105).

DISCUSSION QUESTIONS:

1. Why would Jesus Christ go to the trouble of ensuring the accuracy of the Scriptures?

2. Given the statements of the Lord Jesus Christ and the official teaching of the Episcopal Church about the authority of Scripture, why is it that many in the Church — including even some of her leaders — decry belief in the Bible as "fundamentalism"?

3. How does the historic faith, given once for all, correct us from individual errors and subjectivism?

FOR FURTHER READING:

Bruce, F.F., *The New Testament Documents: Are They Reliable?* William B. Eerdmans.

Packer, James I., *Fundamentalism and the Word of God*, Eerdmans.

Sproul, R.C., *Knowing Scripture*, InterVarsity Press.

Stott, John R.W., *Understanding the Bible*, Zondervan.

Stott, John R.W., *You Can Trust the Bible*, Discovery House Publishers.

6

Taking Time
to Pray

Q. What is prayer?
A. Prayer is responding to God, by thought and by deeds, with or without words.

Q. What is Christian Prayer?
A. Christian prayer is response to God the Father, through Jesus Christ, in the power of the Holy Spirit.[1]

If God were but an impersonal source of power or some impersonal philosophical "truth," conversation with Him would be impossible. In fact, the all-powerful, all-knowing, all-wise, all-loving God of the universe relates to human beings in personal ways. One incredible privilege a disciple has is to enter into relationship with God. Prayer is, at its heart, a conversation with God. We need to spend time with God in prayer.

Jesus' closest followers knew this. While they might have appropriately asked Him, "Lord, teach us to preach" or "Lord, teach us to heal," what they did ask Him was "Lord, teach us to pray (Luke 11:1). They knew what we need to know: We need to spend time with God in prayer.

We need to spend time with God in prayer because He made us to have fellowship with Him. Centuries ago, St. Augustine put it this way: "Thou hast made us for Thyself and our hearts are restless

---

[1]Catechism, *The Book of Common Prayer*, p. 856 sets 4 and 5.

until they find their rest in Thee." A few centuries ago the brilliant French mathematician Blaise Pascal said that we have a God-shaped void within us that only God can fill. The frenzy and the restlessness of people around us stem from their trying to fill that God-shaped void with something other than God. The unfulfilled state that many Church members express comes from a relationship with God that is merely intellectual, cultural or institutional, but not personal.

We need to spend time with God in prayer because we are then likely to become more like Him. In history some people have had encounters with God that are so powerful and dramatic that their faces shone. This was the experience of Moses (Exodus 34:29). While few experience God in such a dramatic way, all Christians can have the experience of a gradual transformation as we spend regular time with the Lord.

Christianity is as much "caught" as it is "taught." We must spend time with the Lord's followers to grow in the Lord's ways. How much more important it is to spend time with the Lord Himself.

We need to spend time with God in prayer so we can learn His will. To be sure, much of God's general will is found in Scripture. In fact, nothing that comes from God to us while we are praying can ever contradict what the Scripture says. Therefore, if there is a clash between what we think we are hearing from God and what the plain meaning of Scripture says, we must always go with Scripture.

But often, the matter at hand is a specific, not a general, question. For example, there is nothing in Scripture about whether the Jones family should move from Massachusetts to New Mexico, or whether Chris Stephenson should be a fireman rather than an electrical engineer, or whether St. Paul's Church should build a new parish hall. Among the various ways we discern God's will is through hearing His voice in prayer.

We need to spend time with God in prayer so we can tell Him what is on our heart. Sometimes this is sin that needs to be confessed and forsaken; sometimes this is an act of rededication to the Lord and His ways; sometimes this is a celebration of joy; sometimes this is a request for God to intervene in our life or in the lives of others.

How do we pray? On the one hand, a quick prayer on the run is always appropriate. Sometimes when I am in a long line at the bank, I'll redeem the time by spending a few minutes in prayer. Sometimes when I hear bad news about someone I love, I'll offer a quick prayer at that moment. Sometimes when I behold a particularly beautiful sunset I'll take a minute to offer praise and adoration to God.

Such quick prayers on the run, while they can be worthy expressions of our relationship with God, are never sufficient in themselves. What we need is a regular time of prayer — daily, focused, and apart from interruptions. I was blessed and challenged by the example of my wife, Mary, during her incredibly busy medical residency a few years ago. No matter how busy she was, she always took time to spend from half an hour to a whole hour in Bible study and prayer each morning. She didn't *find* the time, she *made* the time.

The 18th century New England pastor and scholar Jonathan Edwards said that if he was going to have a busy day, filled with important matters, he'd spend an hour in Bible study and prayer. If he was going to have a *very* busy day, filled with *very* important matters, he'd spend two hours! Edwards knew that while keeping up our part of the relationship with God is a holy obligation, and a spiritual duty on our part, a daily "quiet time" with the Lord is also what makes us become the people God wants us to be and the people we truly want to be. Someone has said that prayer is to the spiritual life what breathing is to the physical life. Therefore, taking the time to pray is the most urgent need in the life of any Christian.

A Framework for Prayer

About 50 years ago the late Canon Clifton A. Best, Canon Missioner of the Episcopal Diocese of Harrisburg/Central Pennsylvania, came up with this framework for daily prayer time. He urged people to try this framework, adapting it as they find helpful. I've adapted his framework and gladly pass it on to you.

Step 1: Concentration. Center your thoughts upon God. Banish distractions. Perhaps gaze on a holy picture, or quietly repeat holy thoughts, such as, "Praise the Lord. Glory to your Holy Name" or "The Lord is God over all the universe" or "Glory to the Father, and to the Son, and to the Holy Spirit; as it was in the beginning, is now, and will be forever. Amen."

Read a portion of Scripture, not so much for the content, but to help focus your thoughts upon God. Confess your sins — penitently — with the intent not to sin in this way again. Ask for His grace to help you live a new life.

> Q. What is penitence?
> A. In penitence, we confess our sins and make restitution where possible, with the intention to amend our lives.[2]

Receive His forgiveness in the light of 1 John 1:9, where God promises, "If we confess our sins, he is faithful and just and will forgive us our sins and purify us from all unrighteousness." Forgive those who have wronged you or your loved ones. If you have trouble doing this, ask God to help you. Close this step by asking God to enable and empower the rest of your prayer time.

Step 2: Meditation. Take a truth of the Christian faith and ponder what it means. Holy pictures or cards with Scripture verses written on them may help. Here are some examples of meditation.

Take a Scripture verse that exhorts people to do something or promises people something and personalize it. For example, in reading John 3:16, "For God so loved the world that he gave his one and only Son, that whoever believes in him shall not perish but have everlasting life," take out the general words and put in your name: "For God so loved Mark that he gave his one and only Son, that Mark, believing in him, shall not perish but have everlasting life." Then take some time to ponder the significance of the personalized passage.

Ponder what Jesus did on the cross — the agony, the shame, the pain. Look, perhaps, at a crucifix or a painting of the crucifixion, or imagine

---

[2]Ibid., p. 857, set 4.

one in your mind. Imagine what that pain would be if it happened to you. Imagine the agony if you watched your child suffer in such a way. Ponder what all of this means spiritually, that God's love is so great that He allowed His Son Jesus to suffer in such a way to pay the penalty for our sins.

Put yourself in a Bible story. Imagine you are the paralyzed man spoken about in the second chapter of the Gospel of Mark. Imagine your friends lowering you through the roof so you can be near Jesus. Then imagine Jesus speaking His words to you about your sin, and then His command that you rise and walk. Imagine what you must be feeling, to be standing on your feet, healed of your paralysis. What joy you must have because you can walk! What love you must have for Jesus! How much to heart have you taken the statement about your forgiveness, glad that your past sins have been forgiven, but careful not to sin again?

Step 3: Adoration. If, through meditation, you are deeply aware of God's blessings for you, His love of you, and of God's presence, then worship and adoration naturally follow.

> Q. What is adoration?
> A. Adoration is the lifting up of the heart and mind to God, asking nothing but to enjoy God's presence.
>
> Q. Why do we praise God?
> A. We praise God, not to obtain anything, but because God's being draws praise from us.[3]

Many express their adoration of God by singing songs of praise; others recite psalms of adoration (Psalm 150 is a good example); others repeat simple praise phrases such as "Hallelujah!" "Praise you Lord" and "I love you Jesus"; others break forth in praise in tongues (see 1 Corinthians 12:8); others sing hymns; others silently bask in quiet adoration of God.

Those who have never experienced a moment of enraptured adoration may wonder what others are talking about when they speak of being "in God's nearer presence." Perhaps an analogy might be the first moments of falling in love. We may have known about our beloved for

---

[3]Ibid., p. 857, sets 1 and 2.

some time. But the first moments of being "in love" are altogether different! Out of that experience comes romantic talk, silly little phrases that mean nothing to those outside the relationship but everything to those in it. Out of that experience comes the basking in each other's presence where simply being together — without saying anything or doing anything — is the most important thing in the world. By analogy, that is what adoration of God is like, our mind beholding the awesome holiness, beauty, and love of God, and our heart being drawn toward Him.

Step 4: Intercession. Simply put, intercession is asking God for something for others.

> Q. What are intercession and petition?
> A. Intercession brings before God the needs of others...that God's will may be done.[4]

We leave this step and the one that follows it until now for two very good reasons. First, because to put prayer requests first most likely means we never go on to anything else in prayer. By following the order of prayer we are putting forth here, we are training ourselves to see God as the Lord Who loves us but Who also has a claim on our lives, rather than as Santa Claus or the Cosmic Delivery Boy, who is around only to do our bidding.

Second, because until we have spent some time concentrating on, contemplating, and adoring God, our requests will be without faith. We are told in Scripture, positively, that faith is important in our receiving God's blessings (Matthew 8:13), and negatively, that its absence can often block blessings from coming our way (Matthew 13:58). Delaying our requests until we have spent some time with God helps us have the necessary faith for when we offer God our requests.

Third, because without spending time with God, we will most likely offer requests that are either inadequate or simply wrong. Sometimes prayer is a nervous reaction rather than a confident trip to the throne of grace. That is, in a moment of crisis someone will offer a prayer for help more as a lucky charm than as an expression of confident trust.

---

[4]Ibid., p. 857, set 6.

Spending time with God can help us to ask correctly. Jesus tells us that we will receive whatever we ask "in my name" (John 14:13). This does not refer to a magic formula — "I want a million dollars *in Jesus' Name. Amen.*" To pray in Jesus' Name means to pray in accordance with His will. We will know His will to the degree we spend time in Scripture and spend time with Him.

Step 5: Petition. This is the time to tell God of your own needs or problems and to ask His help.

> Q. What are intercession and petition?
> A. . . . in petition, we present our own needs, that God's will may be done.[5]

We need to avoid two extremes. One is the attitude that God would never do anything for us because we are too insignificant, too sinful or too mediocre. The fact is, God, in expressing His love, wants to help everyone. To be sure, as He blesses, He also corrects, guides and motivates us. Nevertheless, a whining, defeated prayer like "Please God help me, *if* it be your will" kills faith, and causes us so to look down and not up that we couldn't see, much less receive, the gift that God is trying to hand us.

The other extreme to avoid is the attitude that we can tell God exactly what we want, expecting that if we "claim" it correctly, we will receive it. The truth is, we do not always know how to pray correctly. God forbid that I should receive everything I ask for! In retrospect, I see that some of those things I so wanted would have been very bad for me. Yes, God wants to bless us abundantly, but a cocky, arrogant statement of "I am claiming this right now in Jesus' Name" turns faith into magic, and dethrones God.

We do far better to come to God with our desires and leave them confidently with Him. Often I pray, "Lord, here are my needs as I understand them. I trust you because of Who You are, and because I've seen You at work in my life, in the lives of others, and throughout history. I leave these concerns with You knowing You will answer them — in Your way, in Your time, but always in the way and timing that is best. Lord,

---

[5]Ibid.

if there is something I need to do or stop doing in order to line myself up with Your will better, please show me what that is. I am willing to do my part and I trust You to do Yours. In Jesus' Name. Amen."

Step 6: Thanksgiving. Thank God for Who He is. Thank God for general things. As *The Book of Common Prayer* phrases it (page 58): "We bless thee for our creation, preservation, and all the blessings of this life; but above all for thine inestimable love in the redemption of the world by our Lord Jesus Christ, for the means of grace, and for the hope of glory."

We also thank God for specific blessings He has given us. We thank God in advance for answering those intercessions and petitions we just made. We do that because, although the manner and timing of God's answering them is unknown to us, God will answer every prayer in the way that is just right. So, to thank Him in advance is appropriate.

> Q. For what do we offer thanksgiving?
> A. Thanksgiving is offered to God for all the blessings of this life, for our redemption, and for whatever draws us closer to God.[6]

Step 7: Listening. This is almost always the most neglected step in a time of prayer. We are noisy people! We are more ready to tell God what we want Him to do than to hear what He wants us to do!

This time of silence before the Lord is not passive, but alert and attentive. As Canon Best put it, "Here, in the silence, he gives his ministers their sermons; he gives the Christian physician the right remedy for the sick; to the engineer, answers to his problems; to the chemist, formulas; to the weary, peace; to the sick, healing. Here, too, God reminds us of sins we have yet to confess and forsake, of spiritual duties we are shirking, of responsibilities ignored; he gives us answers to questions, guidance in difficulties, assurance of his love, and true hope for tomorrow."

As we said earlier, never take and run with any purported word that comes from God in prayer. Check out the content of the "message" against Scripture, our final arbiter in matters of faith and morals. Check out any

---

[6]Ibid., p. 857, set 3.

"guidance" or "direction" with other, more mature, Christians. While our walk with God is personal, it is never individualistic. God has put us in a body of Christians to keep us from going off on our own particular tangents.

Finally, what if we have tried all of this and it didn't work? Let's listen to the wise words of the Rev. Edwin Stube: "Don't expect to master all that has been said here the first time you try. Remember the first time you tried to talk to your mother, all you said was, 'Waa.' And though she may have understood fairly well at the time, this is surely not the ultimate in human communication. So our communication with God has not only a beginning, but also a development under his wonderful, patient, loving guidance."

DISCUSSION QUESTIONS:

1. What difference does it make for prayer that God chooses to relate to us personally?

2. Although God already knows our needs, He still wants us to make our requests known to Him. Why?

3. Of the eight steps of prayer, which are easiest for you? Which are hardest?

FOR FURTHER READING:

Brother Lawrence, *The Practice of the Presence of God*, various publishers.

Foster, Richard, *Prayer*, Harper & Row.

7

Knowing God's Will

Q. What response did Christ require?
A. Christ commanded us to believe in Him and to keep His commandments.[1]

As a Christian disciple, isn't your greatest desire to please the Lord Who loves you and died for your sins?

In these confusing, hurried times have you ever wished you could have some sound guidance to help you make decisions?

Most of us likely would say Yes to these questions — but how do we know God's will? The answers to certain timeless questions await us in the pages of Scripture. But where do we turn for particular direction for those matters unique to us? After all, the Bible doesn't say, "Bill, take that job with XYZ Company," or "Susan, you should marry Charles," or "Johnson family, don't buy the property on Adams Street." How do we come to know God's will for our lives in the specific things of today?

Four Basic Predispositions

Before we try to find out God's will for specific questions we need to check to see if we possess the basic predispositions of anyone seeking God's direction:

1. A Yielded Life. The earliest creed recited in the Christian Church

---

[1]Catechism, *The Book of Common Prayer*, p. 851 set 2.

was "Jesus is Lord" (see 1 Corinthians 12:3). God does not reveal Himself to us to satisfy our curiosity; neither does God reveal His will so we may consider it among various options. He is Lord — we must obey. If you ask God for His guidance, you must be ready *in advance* to follow it, no matter what it is. Knowing God's perfect will is a tremendous blessing for a Christian, but it is also a responsibility to carry out.

2. A Patient Heart. The seeker after God's will needs to learn patience and perseverance. God sometimes reveals His will instantaneously, but God often reveals His will over time. We must learn to wait trustfully when God's answers come slowly.

3. A Clear Conscience. Sin separates a person from God just as clouds come between the sun and the earth. Confession of our sins to God removes those "sin clouds" and is necessary to restore the fellowship we must have to receive guidance from God (Psalm 32:1-5, 1 John 1:5-9).

4. An Abiding Spirit. "Be still and know that I am God" (Psalm 46:10). Discerning God's will is not independent of our personal relationship with Him. To know God's will, *we must know Him.* Abiding in Christ (John 15:1-11) by regular prayer, meditation, reading of Scripture, and worship is prerequisite to receiving anything of importance from Him.

Eight Modes of Divine Guidance

I know of eight ways through which God guides us in discovering His will. We needn't use all of these modes when seeking God's guidance, but we will gain greater certainty as we use more of them. Our need for several modes of guidance increases with the importance of our decision.

1. The Word of God. While there are many cases when Scripture gives direct guidance, applicable to all Christians of all cultures and at all times, sometimes there is not such a direct answer for our question. Then we have to find general principles that may apply to our circumstance. For example, when we read "Do not be yoked together with unbelievers" (2 Corinthians 6:14), we may rightly infer God is telling a Christian not to marry a nonbeliever, not to remain in fellowship with a heretical church, or not to go into a business partnership with a nonbeliever.

A word of caution: Lest we go off in an odd direction, using an isolated Bible verse to draw unwarranted conclusions, we must determine what a passage meant in its original context and we must investigate all the Scripture passages pertaining to the matter at hand. After we've done some study we can ask God to show us what it means to our specific situation today. If we come to Scripture prayerfully, God can use general verses to speak to our particular situation.

2. Advice of Other Christians. Others often have the advantage of seeing things less emotionally and more objectively. They may be able to point out something you had not thought of. They may know some relevant Scripture, or have more experience in discerning God's will. Having committed the matter to prayer themselves, they may be able to confirm the decision you are coming to or else state that they disagree and that you should pray more. The advice of a godly pastor is especially helpful.

3. Circumstances. Circumstances often suggest a particular course of action may be right or wrong. God may seem to open a door in a certain direction, or close one in another. For example, someone had been secretly thinking of going into the ordained ministry, but wasn't sure whether God was calling him. Within a week, two people asked, "Have you ever considered the ministry?" Or, a family wants to go on an extended vacation through several states, but lacks money. Out of the blue comes an unexpected inheritance check, covering the expenses of the planned trip.

If we are truly willing to obey, God will open and close doors through circumstances. We need to keep our spiritual eyes attuned so we will correctly understand the circumstances. We will soon learn that what we once considered *coincidental* events are sometimes *providential* events.

4. Common sense. We should not overlook common sense — investigating, checking, and making use of the common wisdom and understanding available to us as human beings. For example, you feel the Lord is leading you to buy a particular used car. Common sense says you should have it thoroughly checked out by a good mechanic so you won't waste the Lord's money on a lemon.

There are two objections often raised when one mentions common sense. One is that since the human mind is corrupted by sin (Romans 1:28; 2 Corinthians 3:14-6, 4:4), common sense is not trustworthy. But why should Holy Spirit-assisted common sense be corrupted any more than any other part of us, like our ability to pray or read the Bible? When the Holy Spirit takes control of us, our common sense is — with everything else — in the process of renewal. In the Holy Spirit it is possible to have "Sanctified Common Sense" (see Romans 12:2).

The second objection is that using common sense is to walk by sight, not by faith. This is a misapplication of that Scriptural statement. Jesus told of the foolishness of some who started building a tower before they calculated the number of bricks on hand and had to quit in the middle of the project (Luke 14:28-30).

God often wants us to use our common sense in determining a course of action, *but not always.* Sometimes God commands what is foolish in the eyes of the world or even in our own eyes. I know of a family whom God told to sell their home, pack their possessions in a trailer and head south until He told them to stop. It led to a very fruitful ministry and happiness for the entire family. Make use, then, of common sense, but listen for when God overrules it.

5. Prophecy. Prophecy, in this context, is God speaking directly to His people today about specific situations through another person exercising the spiritual gift called prophecy (see 1 Corinthians 12:10). Sometimes in prayer meetings, worship services, or sessions of one-on-one ministry, people will speak words they believe have come directly from God. These words are not their own wisdom or thoughts, but are given directly from God for a group or a specific individual. Often the one speaking these words does not understand how the message has direct application or even makes sense.

Years ago I believed God wanted me to do graduate theological study in Oxford, England. Nevertheless, I felt some fears and a little bit of uncertainty. What if I was wrong in my discernment of God's will? This was too important a decision to err in. About that time, I went to a prayer meeting and someone whom I had never met stood up on the other side of the room and said something like, "Get thee off to a far off country and dwell there with my people for my Name's sake." A warm feeling came over me as she spoke. I felt assured that God was indeed directing me to study in England. After that evening I never again felt anxious or uncertain about the decision.

6. "Laying Out a Fleece." Gideon in the Old Testament wanted to know whether God would deliver Israel from the hand of Midian (Judges 6:36-40). He laid out a fleece (a sheep's skin), asking God to make the fleece wet and the ground dry if God was, indeed, going to deliver Israel.

If we are unsure of a particular course of action, we can ask God for a sign by saying, "If you want me to do this, I ask that such-and-such will happen by such-and-such a time." We call this "laying out a fleece." Early in his ministry, Billy Graham was uncertain whether he should preach on the radio. Graham announced to a crusade meeting that he needed funds to buy air time, and he secretly asked God for $25,000 by midnight. Graham trusted that if God wanted him on the air the money would be there, but if not, the money would be short of the goal. By midnight Graham had raised slightly more than $25,000, and his radio ministry began shortly thereafter.

God allows us to make use of this means of guidance from time to time, but our constant seeking of such signs displeases Him (Matthew 12:38-9, John 4:48). Laying out conditions for God to fulfill can be a sign of laziness. We may be looking for a quick, easy answer, rather than thinking through and praying through an issue.

In addition, too constant a use of "laying out a fleece" can usurp God's honor by insisting He follow our tests and whims rather than our patiently waiting upon His voice. Even Gideon was pushing things when He laid out His fleece, for God had already clearly told him what the results of the forthcoming battle would be and had confirmed it with a miraculous sign (Judges 6:14-22). Remember, once you have set the conditions of the fleece (in Billy Graham's case, $25,000 by midnight), do not change them if things don't seem to work out the way you want.

7. Feeling Led. Many people pray over issues and feel strongly pushed in one direction or another. We believe that we are led by God and not our own desires, so when someone asks us why we undertook a certain action, we respond, "I feel God led me."

We must be careful in this area of guidance more than in any other. Some people reject the whole idea of "feeling led" as someone's emotions playing tricks. Other people think they see God's guiding hand in every thought or feeling that comes to them. Both positions are too extreme.

To those who discount the whole idea of "feeling led" I would say this: years ago, when I was a newly ordained parish priest and out visiting parishioners, I would get the strongest urge to drop in on a certain family. Often, when they greeted me at the door, they would say, "Thank you for stopping by. I was praying God would lead you here. I just got some terrible news." This didn't happen all the time, nor did its occasional occurrence take away my need to plan a regular course of visiting, but it happened more frequently than might be expected were it just coincidence.

Someone I know felt led all of a sudden to pull her car over to the side of the road. She didn't know why she should do this other than the strong feeling that God was telling her to do it. She soon found out the reason when a large tree fell across the very spot where she would have been driving.

On occasion, St. Paul felt God's guidance about where he should preach (Acts 16:6-10). He suggests it is a part of spiritual life to be led and perceive God's leading within ourselves (Romans 8:14; Galatians 5:18). The more we grow as Christians, the more we should expect to perceive God moving us in one direction or another and to discern those feelings correctly.

To those who use this mode of guidance, a word of caution: Feelings of "I felt the Lord led me" are among the most easily confused means of guidance. We can easily confuse personal desires or unresolved emotional wounds as God's guidance.

Many times people have felt strongly that a particular feeling or "leading" was from God, only to discover their error later. To announce constantly to people that God told you this or the Spirit led you to that could become a dangerous form of pride and the worst sort of taking the Lord's Name in vain. It might hold the Lord's Name up to mockery by nonbelievers and be a discouragement and disillusionment to believers to hear that God said something, only to retract the statement later.

If you believe God is leading you (and especially if you are going to announce it publicly and involve other people), make sure you have wrestled with the matter *thoroughly* in prayer, and have sought God's guidance by several of the modes of guidance listed here. This word of warning is necessary, but don't let it paralyze you. Act responsibly on your understanding of God's guidance. It is often by trial-and-error that we learn to distinguish between our own human emotions and God's prompting.

8. The Peace of Christ. St. Paul exhorts us to let the peace of Christ rule in our hearts (Colossians 3:15). The Greek word translated as rule means to "be an arbiter or umpire." The final consideration of whether we should do something is whether we have peace about it. This does not necessarily mean we aren't scared; it means we know the decision is the correct one. I know many people who were very unsure on their wedding day about what sort of life awaited them, but they had peace that the decision was the correct one.

Some Further Considerations

We should apply a few other considerations in deciding whether a decision is of the Lord.

1. Is it an action that would produce good or bad fruit? God's ways are ways of love and peace; Satan's ways are ways of hate and turmoil.

While there is a godly kind of anger, there is a kind of anger that is not (see Ephesians 4:26). No action can be of God if it does not produce His fruit (Galatians 5:22-3).

2. Does an action give glory to God, or would God be ashamed of it? If there is praise or credit involved, are we self-seeking or God-glorifying (John 12:43, 1 Corinthians 10:31)?

3. Am I rationalizing my actions? Am I really discerning God's guidance, or am I piously justifying what I want to do?

4. Would I be embarrassed if Jesus were present? If I could not do the planned action with Jesus present, I had better stop immediately, for He is *always* present (Matthew 28:20).

5. Does it hurt or enhance my spiritual development?

6. Does it lead another person away from Christ or cause that person to stumble? St. Paul said he would never do anything to cause another to fall (Romans 14:13; 1 Corinthians 8:9-13).

7. Does it involve denying the clear, simple meaning of Scripture?

8. Does it involve compromising the truth? No blessing ever comes by our taking shortcuts with God. May God fill you "with the knowledge of His will in all spiritual wisdom and understanding, to lead a life worthy of the Lord, fully pleasing to Him, bearing fruit in every good work, and increasing in the knowledge of God" (Colossians 1:9-10).

DISCUSSION QUESTIONS:

1. In facing a serious decision, have you ever used the various modes of discerning God's will as described in this chapter? How did this process work for you?

2. Our human desires often subtly steer us away from discerning God's will. What can we do about this problem?

3. What do you say when a person enthusiastically declares, "God told me . . ."?

FOR FURTHER READING:

Elliot, Elisabeth, *The Liberty of Obedience*, Servant Books.

Smith, M., *Knowing God's Will*, InterVarsity Press.

Stanley, Charles, *How to Know God's Will*, NavPress.

8

The Church

Q. What is the Church?
A The Church is the community of the New Covenant.

Q. How is the Church described in the Bible?
A. The Church is described as the Body of which Jesus Christ is the Head and of which all baptized persons are members. It is called the People of God, the New Israel, a holy nation, a royal priesthood, and the pillar and ground of truth.[1]

In the last three chapters we have examined three responsibilities of the individual Christian, namely studying Scripture, practicing prayer, and seeking God's will. We now must turn to another aspect of responsible Christian discipleship: being an active participant in the Body of Christ, the Church.

The New Testament provides us with several rich metaphors for the Church. Scripture calls Christians "members of his body" (1 Corinthians 12:27), "sheep of Christ's flock" (John 10:14-16), "branches of his vine" (John 15:1-8), and "stones in his temple" (Ephesians 2:19-22).

Not only are believers one with Christ through His Church, they are one with countless numbers of brothers and sisters. For the many people in society who experience a longing for God, here is a community where, despite its faults and failures, one can find God and enter into a rich, personal relationship with Him. For the many people in society

---

[1]Catechism, *The Book of Common Prayer*, p. 854, sets 1 and 2.

who feel isolated and alienated, here is a community where, despite its faults and failures, there is love and acceptance. For the many people in society who believe they have no purpose in life, here is a community where, despite its faults and failures, people are working together to make a difference in the world.

In spite of the rich blessings participation in the Church brings, many Christians believe the Church is only a necessary evil. Many others do not even believe it is necessary at all. As one man told me, "Jesus I like. The Church I can do without." Such an attitude is understandable. The Church always falls far short of her calling as the spotless Bride of Christ. We all know those who affiliate with the Church for reasons other than obedience to Christ. In addition, we have all seen the hypocrisy and we have all witnessed the scandals that have befallen some Church leaders.

Even when the Church is better than this, it is still far too often tedious and boring. So many people ask, "Who needs it?" C.S. Lewis expressed this sentiment in his usual straightforward way: "Though I liked clergymen as I liked bears, I had as little wish to be in the church as in the zoo. . . . To me, religion ought to have been a matter of good men praying alone and meeting by twos and threes to talk of spiritual matters." So why, then, should we be active, intentional participants in the Church?

It is the will of Christ. Our Lord made provision for a Church to carry on His work once He ascended back to Heaven. We see this in His three-year apprenticeship of those who would become the Church's leadership. We see this in the Father's sending the Holy Spirit at Pentecost so they might continue the mighty works Jesus did (John 14:12). We see this in Jesus' inauguration of the Lord's Supper, a communal meal to be continued until His return (Luke 22:14-20; 1 Corinthians 11:23-26.) We see this in Jesus' instructing His followers to pray *Our* Father Who art in Heaven, not just *my* Father (Matthew 6:9).

It helps rule out individual quirks of Christian understanding and expression. While each Christian can know much about the things of the Lord, we know only in part (1 Corinthians 13:9). While sometimes our individual quirks of spirituality are harmless (and often amusing), on some occasions they can be quite harmful, both to our own spiritual growth and to that of others. Being part of the Church helps to keep us from falling into such individualistic quirks. As we submit ourselves and our ideas to the larger Christian community, we are much more likely to be on solid ground spiritually. The wise counsel of mature Christians — in our own congregation, in the wider Church, and throughout the centuries — keeps us in balance. Mature Christians often disagree about minor points of belief and practice. On more substantive matters there is usually a wonderful *consensus of the faithful*, something we neglect to our peril.

It places us on a team where all the necessary gifts for ministry are present. According to Scripture, each person possesses one or more of the gifts of the Holy Spirit for ministry (1 Corinthians 12:7). Similarly, no one possesses them all. If we remain generally isolated from other Christians we will rise only to the level of our own giftedness. We will not be able to receive the ministry of others where we remain weak. By being and working together we offer a full, rich, complete ministry to others and enjoy its benefits ourselves. We offer our own particular gifts for the greater good, and we receive what we need from others.

It helps knock off our rough edges. Solo Christianity may help us avoid dealing with unpleasant aspects of who we are, but there is no growth or challenge in such avoidance. By being part of a community we are constantly confronted with areas in which we need to grow. Sometimes this challenge comes as others hold us accountable. Their words — whether gentle or sharp — point out to us where we still fall short. Sometimes we see our need as we personally reflect on our attitudes and behaviors in our relationships with others. Having to work on our shortcomings is not always pleasant, but it is necessary if we are to become mature as people and as Christians.

It is where we receive the sacraments. While the sacraments are not the only ways God blesses His people, they are important means of grace generally necessary for the health of our souls. God entrusted these sacraments to the Christian community, and the community carries them out.

For these reasons and more, we are to be active, intentional participants in the Church. It is not an option. As the famous saying puts it, "If you do not have the Church for your mother, you do not have God for your Father." As John Wesley once said, "To turn Christianity into a solitary religion is to destroy it."

Q. Why is the Church described as holy?

A. The Church is holy, because the Holy Spirit dwells in it, consecrates its members, and guides them to do God's work.

Q. Why is the Church described as apostolic?

A. The Church is apostolic, because it continued in the teaching and fellowship of the apostles and is sent to carry out Christ's mission to all people.[2]

Because the Church consists of people, it will always fall short of the ideal of teaching and living the faith as taught in Scripture. No local congregation or the denomination of which it is a part is perfect. When your local congregation or denomination falls short of what Christ would have it be, prayerfully and humbly work to help it. You have no more right to abandon them for their shortcomings than you do to abandon your family members when they let you down. And remember, you are not perfect yourself. Part of the problem of the Church is *you*, so let others minister to you that you too will grow.

Nevertheless, if your congregation or denomination has significantly departed from the clear teaching of Scripture, or refuses to change its unscriptural policies or practices even after repeated entreaties from believers, or fails to discipline heretical or immoral members, it may be necessary to leave for a church community that desires to remain true to Christ.

How can the Church reflect the holiness of God if its members do not intend to be a holy people obeying what God has commanded? How can the Church offer an alternative to the world if the Church acts just like the world? How can the Church say to those who are sick of their sin that transformation by the Lord is possible if it does not demand its members grow in holiness and assist them in that task?

---

[2]Ibid., p. 854, sets 5 and 7.

Scripture tells us that those who persist in immoral practices must be disciplined (Matthew 18:15-17 and 1 Corinthians 5:1-11). A church that refuses to discipline, or commends such practices as "alternative lifestyles," departs from its divine calling. If such a church will not return to the ways of Christ after we plead with it repeatedly, we may have to abandon it.

DISCUSSION QUESTIONS:

1. Why do you think Jesus set up the Church and wants Christian believers to be a part of it?

2. How has the Church been a source of blessing to you over the years?

3. What do you like most about the local congregation of which you are a part?

4. What do you like least?

5. What would cause you to leave your local congregation or your denomination?

FOR FURTHER READING:

Watson, David, *I Believe in the Church*, Eerdmans.

9

The Eucharist (or Holy Communion)

Q. What are the sacraments?

A. The sacraments are outward and visible signs of inward and spiritual grace, given by Christ as sure and certain means by which we receive grace.

Q. What is grace?

A. Grace is God's favor towards us, unearned and undeserved; by grace God forgives our sins, enlightens our minds, stirs our hearts, and strengthens our wills.

Q. What is the Holy Eucharist?

A. The Holy Eucharist is the sacrament commanded by Christ for the continual remembrance of his life, death, and resurrection, until his coming again.

Q. What is the outward and visible sign in the Eucharist?

A. The outward and visible sign in the Eucharist is bread and wine, given and received according to Christ's command.

Q. What is the inward and spiritual grace given in the Eucharist?

A. The inward and spiritual grace in the Holy Communion is the Body and Blood of Christ given to his people, and received by faith.

Q. What are the benefits which we receive in the Lord's Supper?

A. The benefits we receive are the forgiveness of our sins, the strengthening of our union with Christ and one another, and the foretaste of the heavenly banquet which is our nourishment in eternal life.[1]

Nearly all Christian denominations believe the chief expression of worship by and fellowship among Christians is the Holy Eucharist, also called Holy Communion, the Divine Liturgy, the Mass, or the Lord's

---

[1]Catechism, *The Book of Common Prayer*, p. 857, set 8; p. 858, set 1; 859, set 1, 4, 5 and 6.

Supper. Jesus instituted this sacrament on Thursday evening of Holy Week, His last evening on earth.

From the earliest days of the Church, the Holy Eucharist was the way Christians worshiped on Sunday. Luke tells us that in Asia Minor around A.D. 57 churches gathered on Sunday "to break bread" (Acts 20:7). Justin Martyr, a church leader in the second century A.D., wrote this description of Sunday worship in his "First Apology" (about A.D. 155):

> On the day which is called Sunday, all who live in the cities or in the countryside gather together in one place. And the memoirs of the apostles or the writings of the prophets are read as long as there is time. Then, when the reader is finished, the president, in a discourse, admonishes the people to practice these examples of virtue. Then we all stand together and offer prayers. And . . . [then] bread is presented, and wine with water. . . . The elements which have been "eucharistized" are distributed and received by each one; and they are sent to the absent by the deacons.

If the earliest Christians centered their worship in the Eucharist, why then did "Morning Prayer" or "Morning Worship" — services of prayer and sermon but not Holy Communion — become the standard fare in so many churches?

1. Reaction to Catholicism. In the Middle Ages various superstitions arose concerning the elements of Holy Communion. Some people buried consecrated wafers in their fields as insurance for good harvests. Some people carried a wafer as a good luck charm. In reaction to such superstition, and to such woeful ignorance of the Scriptures, many Protestant reformers stressed preaching and downplayed Holy Communion. Many Protestants since that time, in reaction to or even in prejudice of "Catholic things," have relegated Communion to an inferior status.

2. "Scientific" Rationalism. This philosophy, prevalent since the so-called Enlightenment of 350 years ago, says that the only things proven are the things one can prove scientifically. While many Christians have overcome this worldview sufficiently to believe in our Lord's supernatural birth and resurrection, they have not always overcome this worldview sufficiently to believe that the Communion is anything more than a mere memorial. When, however, Christians understand the Communion to be a means of grace, able to bless, empower, transform and heal, they want it much more frequently. Until they do, they deem it merely a visual aid and, therefore, one they need infrequently.

3. The frontier. When John Wesley was a student at Oxford, he received Holy Communion four times a week. Later, however, as many Methodist circuit-riding preachers fanned out into the American frontier, they did not (or could not) follow Wesley's example. Many of these circuit-riders were lay preachers, unauthorized to preside at the Holy Communion. By the time each congregation received its own resident, ordained pastor, the custom of infrequent Holy Communion was established.

4. Lazy spirituality. Scripture tells us we should not go to Holy Communion unprepared (1 Corinthians 11:27-30).

> Q. What is required of us when we come to the Eucharist?
> A. It is required that we should examine our lives, repent of our sins, and be in love and charity with all people.[2]

For, as the benefit is great, if with penitent hearts and living faith we receive the holy Sacrament, so is the danger great, if we receive it improperly, not recognizing the Lord's Body.[3]

In Geneva, Switzerland, during the time of the Protestant Reformation, Church leaders examined people individually before they could receive Communion. Because this took work by parishioners, many wanted Communion (and its requisite preparation) less often!

Why should we, then, desire that Holy Communion be the regular Sunday service in our churches if it isn't already? Why should we thank God for this opportunity to receive it at least weekly if not more frequently?

1. Because it seems to be what God wants. The early Church knew this, and people of all denominations, as they grow in Christ, often instinctively perceive the need for a more regular feeding at the Lord's Table. Note, for example, how so many of those congregations that celebrated the Holy Communion quarterly are now offering it monthly, and how many that observed it monthly are moving to a twice-monthly or even weekly observance.

---

[2]Ibid., p. 860, set 1.
[3]From "An Exhortation," *The Book of Common Prayer*, p. 316.

2. Because we need God to feed us in ways in addition to the rational. It is good that we are fed intellectually as we hear God's Word read and taught. It is also good to be fed sacramentally and mystically in the Holy Communion. Christianity, while not irrational, is not merely rational. God speaks to our minds through the truths embodied in Scripture. God also speaks to our innermost beings in ways beyond our understanding. In Luke 24:30-31 we read how two of Jesus' disciples finally recognized the man in their midst to be Jesus as He broke bread with them.

3. Because God uses material means to convey spiritual blessings. In the Incarnation, God (Who is spirit) took human flesh. Jesus does not just *symbolize* God in our midst, He *is* God in our midst in human form. Therefore, we should not find it difficult to believe that God can use material means to convey spiritual blessings. In the sacraments, God uses outward and visible signs to work inward and spiritual blessings. The signs are not just symbols — any more than Jesus was just a symbol of God. The sacraments convey the blessings that they illustrate. We do not want to push this point into an imbalance — that our inward spiritual disposition and our careful preparation for receiving the sacraments are unimportant. Nevertheless, I find it reassuring to know that God can meet me in the sacraments even on those days when my faith is weak, my mind and heart are confused, or my ability to do my part is lessened.

Having fed on the rich blessings of the Eucharist and having been empowered by it, we can then confidently pray to the Lord for Him to "send us out to do the work you have given us to do, to love and serve you as faithful witnesses of Christ our Lord."[4]

DISCUSSION QUESTIONS:

1. Has your appreciation for the sacraments grown over the years? If so, how? What helped this occur?

2. How do you prepare for receiving Holy Communion?

3. Are you aware of a specific blessing — such as a healing, a new awareness of God, a vision of God or an angel, a "weight" being lifted from you, a spiritual insight — happening while, or immediately after, receiving Holy Communion?

---

[4]*The Book of Common Prayer*, p. 366.

FOR FURTHER READING:

Scanlan, Michael, and Shields, Ann Therese, *And Their Eyes Were Opened — Encountering Jesus in the Sacraments*, Servant Publications.

Pearson, Mark A., *Christian Healing: A Practical, Comprehensive Guide*, Chosen Books. (See especially Chapter 9, which discusses the relationship of the sacraments to the Christian healing ministry.)

10

Evangelism:
Telling *The* Story and Telling *Our* Story

Q. What is the mission of the Church?
A. The mission of the Church is to restore all people to unity with God and each other in Christ.

Q. Through whom does the Church carry out its mission?
A. The Church carries out its mission through the ministry of all its members.[1]

William Temple, Archbishop of Canterbury during the Second World War, wrote what is perhaps the best definition of evangelism. The General Convention of the Episcopal Church adopted this statement in 1973 as our Church's official definition of evangelism:

"Evangelism is the presentation of Jesus Christ in the power of the Holy Spirit, in such ways that persons may be led to believe in him as Saviour and follow him as Lord within the fellowship of the Church."

Whether talking with the rich young ruler (Luke 18:18-30), a Jewish leader like Nicodemus (John 3:1-21), or the woman at the well (John 4:4-38), Jesus sought to win people to salvation through trust in Him. The Father sent Him to bear witness. Jesus said that just as the Father sent Him, He sends us (John 20:21). In short, Jesus wants us to tell others about Him and lead them into mature discipleship (Matthew 28:19-20).

---

[1]Catechism, *The Book of Common Prayer*, p. 855, sets 1 and 3.

Motive

The motive for evangelism is three-fold.

First, to obey the Lord. He told us to evangelize. Therefore, followers of Jesus will do it. It's that simple.

Second, to present people with the greatest, most important news there is. Jesus made it abundantly and repeatedly clear that there are two final, eternal resting places — heaven and hell. He told parables of the wise and foolish virgins and how the latter group was locked out permanently (Matthew 25:1-13); of the wheat harvested and the weeds burned (Matthew 13:24-30, 36-43); of the sheep kept and the goats sent away into eternal punishment (Matthew 25:31-46); of the good fish kept and the bad fish thrown away (Matthew 13:47-50); of two in one bed with one taken and the other left behind (Luke 17:34); of two women grinding meal together with one taken and the other left behind (Luke 17:35); and of Lazarus eternally safe in the bosom of Abraham and the rich man in torment (Luke 16:19-31).

The doctrine of eternal life and eternal lostness is not based on one isolated reference, nor is it some Old Testament teaching replaced by the "more compassionate teaching" of the New Testament, nor is it an idea mentioned only by an Epistle writer. Rather it is the clear, repeated teaching of Jesus. Therefore, we must reject the popular but erroneous teaching that everyone is going to heaven. The Gospel is the good news that eternally lost sinners can be reconciled with God through the atoning work of Jesus Christ. The bad news is that apart from a personal, saving relationship with Jesus Christ, no one will go to heaven.

> Q. What do we mean by heaven and hell?
> A. By heaven, we mean eternal life in our enjoyment of God; by hell, we mean eternal death in our rejection of God.[2]

The third motive for evangelism is to offer to people the things they need for a quality life now: forgiveness, a purpose in life, guidance, help in overcoming those traits in themselves they know to be harmful, a stable source of truth, and divine intervention at points of need.

---

[2]Ibid., p. 862, set 2.

Telling the Story

We have already looked at the contents of Gospel in some detail (see Chapter 1). This Gospel is objectively true for people regardless of race, gender, education, culture, income, or occupation. The Gospel is the story that leads people to Christ, Who saves people for all eternity and offers other blessings here on earth. This basic message is of primary importance, more important than witnessing to the particular blessings or miracles we have received. The reason for this is simple. If we do not share the objective, basic Gospel message, our listeners may attribute God's work to luck, coincidence, or something that He chose to do just for us. How will they know that blessings can happen to them as well unless we point to the objective, true-for-everyone promises of the Gospel?

In addition, our purpose is not primarily to lead people to *experiences* of God, or temporal blessings from God, however wonderful they are. Our *first* priority is to lead people to Jesus as Lord and Saviour. If we talk only of healings, blessings or exciting spiritual experiences, people might desire *those experiences* rather than humble themselves as sinners in need of salvation. As Jesus taught, there is no ultimate point to gaining the world while losing one's soul (Matthew 6:33, 16:26). So, then, the greatest importance is sharing the basic message of the Gospel. (If you're uncertain about the Gospel, revisit the basic Gospel message outlined in Chapter 1.)

But in addition to the basic Gospel message there is a place for telling our own story by giving examples of how God has worked in our own lives. If we don't tell people the difference God made in our lives, the Gospel message will sound academic and remote, unrelated to daily life and its many problems. For example, some who are physically hungry cannot hear about spiritual food until they have eaten lunch.

What are the kinds of things we share? While there are so many different things God does in a person's life — "innumerable benefits," as *The Book of Common Prayer* puts it — we should focus on sharing those blessings most like the perceived or felt needs of our listeners. To put it in plain language, we need to "scratch them where they itch." Or, as a friend of mine says, "Put the cookies on the bottom shelf." We need to listen carefully and lovingly to their hurts, fears, aspirations, and hopes and tell them how Jesus has helped us in similar areas. Such responding to felt needs is how Jesus started sharing the Good News with many people.

Here are just a few of the things we can share about what God does in people's lives:

1. God helps people know Him in a personal way. You may remember from a few chapters ago the statements from St. Augustine ("Thou hast made us for Thyself and our hearts are restless until they find their rest in Thee") and Blaise Pascal (the "God-shaped void" within us). Some people know their hearts are restless but they may not know the source of this restlessness. Some people are not aware of their God-shaped void and wonder, despite their accomplishments, why they are not satisfied with life. Others know there is a God and want desperately to have fellowship with Him but do not know how to find God. Others know there is a "god" but their beliefs about God are significantly different from God as He has revealed Himself.

Our witness to such people is to tell them how we have come to know God and how His presence within us has given our hearts rest and filled the void made only for Him. Perhaps we can share how we, too, had a sense that "something was missing" and found out that it was God. Be careful, however, not to give the impression that you have a special hotline to God that few others have, or that your relationship with the Lord is more intimate than it really is, or that your life is free from struggles. This kind of witnessing turns people off rather than attracting them to God.

2. God helps people who have real problems. God said to Moses, "Thus shall you say to the house of Jacob, and tell the people of Israel: 'You have seen what I did to the Egyptians, and how I bore you on eagles' wings and brought you to myself'" (Exodus 19:3-4). The same God Who delivered the children of Israel through the hand of Moses still delivers people from their bondages and problems today. We can share how God has done this in our experience.

One word of caution, however. Sometimes God does indeed deliver a person (or a family) from a problem by removing that problem. Other times, He gives people grace to triumph in the midst of the problem that still remains (as St. Paul found out; see the end of Romans 8). While both are wonderful, we could set people up for disillusionment if we give them the impression that God's help with problems always means He will take the problems away.

3. God changes our inner disposition and changes the way we act toward others. Accounts of how God has changed us are important to share. You can share some examples of how God works deep within us, such as: (a) giving us peace when our outward circumstances are conducive to turmoil instead; (b) helping us bear no bitterness toward someone who has harmed us; (c) taking away our propensity toward jealousy; (d) helping us to let go and trust others when keeping rigid control was our normal way of life.

Many people want to do the right thing and feel frustrated that it is difficult to do. Many more people want to be at peace within themselves. Our stories of how God has worked changes within us are testimonies people want to hear, provided these testimonies ring true. Few people believe those testimonies that say we were 100 percent awful beforehand and are 100 percent perfect now. It never helps to exaggerate! Simply describe how God has helped you thus far and how you still need God's help in the constant process of growth. In addition, people will not believe our words if our actions contradict them. When they do see something appealing in us that is a work of God's transforming grace, we can share that this is an action of the Lord.

4. God heals the sick. Whether dramatically or quietly, instantaneously or gradually, with the help of medicine or by a direct intervention from on high, a major physical illness or a lifelong emotional problem stemming from childhood abuse, God heals today. If we have received a healing from God or if we have been an eyewitness to one, we can share this.

Again, a word of caution. We do not help God by saying anything beyond what actually happened. A healing that occurred gradually is not less an example of God at work. We need not be ashamed of sharing that kind of healing. Nor is it robbing God of the glory to say that some of our healing may be due to medicine or counseling. These are instruments God invented and uses. If we deny this truth, our witness will not ring true and our witnessing may be counterproductive.[3]

How Do We Share?

We should remember several guidelines as we share either the message of the Gospel or our personal witness with others:

1. Rely on the Holy Spirit for assistance. First, ask the Spirit to send opportunities to witness. Sometimes at the beginning of the day I will pray, "Dear God, send me someone today who wants to know about You and with whom I may share the Gospel." Often that is exactly what happens. Second, by asking the Holy Spirit to give us the words to say. We fear evangelism because we are afraid we will become tongue-tied or make fools of ourselves and of God. By asking the Holy Spirit to give us the words, we can trust that God — Who wants people to come to Him far more than we ever will — will help us when we are sharing. We can ask God for His help ahead of time and we can pray silently while we are in the middle of sharing with others.

2. Be gentle. If the Holy Spirit is not at work in the person with whom we are witnessing, nothing real and lasting will take place, no matter how clever or earnest we are. If the Holy Spirit is at work, we need not try to do His job for Him, but we do need to do ours. Our job is to bear witness to the Gospel — the message God has for everyone and how it has worked in our life. It is the Spirit's job to convince the other person (John 16:7-11). Witnessing to others about the Lord, therefore, is a cooperative venture. As Jesus put it, "when the Counselor comes . . . He will bear witness to me; and you are my witnesses" (John 15:26-27).

3. Listen for "openings." People are constantly giving us openings to share our faith, but seldom do they state their interest in theological

---

[3]For more information on how God heals today, see my book *Christian Healing: A Practical, Comprehensive Guide* (Chosen Books).